J. Y. Sargent

Grammar of the Dano-Norwegian language

J. Y. Sargent

Grammar of the Dano-Norwegian language

ISBN/EAN: 9783743394155

Manufactured in Europe, USA, Canada, Australia, Japa

Cover: Foto ©Paul-Georg Meister /pixelio.de

Manufactured and distributed by brebook publishing software (www.brebook.com)

J. Y. Sargent

Grammar of the Dano-Norwegian language

GRAMMAR

OF

DANO-NORWEGIAN LANGUAGE

BY

J. Y. SARGENT, M.A.

FELLOW OF HERTFORD COLLEGE

Oxford
AT THE CLARENDON PRESS
1892

Oxford
PRINTED AT THE CLARENDON PRESS
BY HORACE HART, PRINTER TO THE UNIVERSITY

PREFACE

THE present work is based on the 'Outlines of Norwegian Grammar,' by the same author, published in 1865. At that time the number of English travellers in Norway was comparatively small. Most of them were accustomed to make a considerable sojourn in the country each year, for the sake of fishing and shooting, and, living as they did among a population speaking only the native language, they felt the want of some manual conveying just sufficient knowledge of the rudiments to enable them to interpret or construct a sentence on correct grammatical lines.

To supply this need I prepared a short Grammar, giving so much information as was necessary to lay a foundation, and no more. This book has been long out of print, having, I believe, fulfilled the purpose for which it was written.

Since then the crowd of English and Americans visiting Norway every summer has greatly increased; and although the majority of these, being mere tourists, do not feel any necessity for learning the language, yet there are many among them who would gladly qualify themselves to be their own interpreters.

But over and above these summer visitors, there is a large

and growing class in England and America, who, either for business purposes, or from curiosity to know something of the Norse language and literature, would prefer to learn the language at home, and to study at their leisure the writings of Danish and Norwegian authors; and to these a Grammar is almost indispensable.

To meet the additional requirements of such students it seemed necessary to treat the subject more systematically, entering into fuller details, and noticing exceptional and idiomatic usages, reference to which might be safely omitted as long as the object was only to instruct the learner how to frame a question intelligibly, and to understand the syntax of an answer.

Accordingly I have remodelled the book, without however departing from the ordinary grammatical method, which is most generally known and easiest to follow. Thus I have given (1) a short account of the Form and Sound of the Letters; (2) Rules for the Inflection of the several Parts of speech; (3) the Syntax of sentences simple and compound, so far as the Dano-Norwegian idiom differs from the English, or seems to deserve especial attention for any other reason.

But Rules without Examples are like skeletons without flesh; just as Examples without Rules, as they are presented to us in Conversational Manuals, are no better than dried specimens, having no principle of growth in them.

Therefore each rule with its exceptions, and the general as well as the special use of each part of speech, have been illustrated by one or more examples. Besides the quotations and illustrations, appropriate to the several rules,

PREFACE. vii

a List of miscellaneous phrases, proverbial sayings, and idioms, taken, like the former, from the every-day language of the people, together with samples of Epistolary formulæ, and a specimen of some Norwegian peculiarities of spelling and pronunciation, has been added for the benefit of those whose chief and special object is to learn to talk in the Dano-Norwegian tongue.

In composing the present edition I have consulted and derived help, which I thankfully acknowledge, from several works published since the appearance of my earlier book. Among them are the following: Dansk-Norsk-Engelsk Ordbog, by A. Larsen, Copenhagen; Norsk Ordbog med Dansk Forklaring. I. Aasen, Christiania; Udvalg af norske og danske Forfattere, A. E. Erikson, Christiania; Norsk Grammatik til Skolebrug, S. W. Hofgaard, Christiania; Modersmaalets Grammatik, J. Løkke, Christiania; Brev og Formularbog, Christiania; Engelske Samtale-øvelser. J. T. Bendeke and G. Stabell, Trondhjem; Engelsk Grammatik for Middelskolen, A. Western, Christiania.

For a general revision of the sheets I am indebted to the kindness of Sir Henry Pottinger, my friend and comrade during many seasons in Scandinavia, whose sound judgment and thorough acquaintance with the language of Norway have afforded many useful suggestions, and diminished the number of mistakes.

J. Y. S.

July, 1892.

CONTENTS

LETTERS.

	PAGE
Alphabet, Form of	1
Orthography	2
Sound of Vowels	2
,, Diphthongs	4
,, Consonants	4
Remarks on Pronunciation	6
Phonetic Examples	8

WORDS.

Accidence. Introductory.

Parts of Speech	9
Number	9
Case	9
Gender	9
Inflection	9

ARTICLES.

Articles	11
Indefinite Article	11
Definite Article	11
Definite Article with Substantives	11
,, with Adjectives	11
Remarks on the Articles	12
Examples of use of the Articles	14

SUBSTANTIVES.

	PAGE
Gender of Substantives	16
Case	16
Number	16
Declension	16
Paradigm of 1st Declension	16
„ of 2nd Declension	17
„ of 3rd Declension	17
„ of 4th Declension	17
Declension with Vowel change	18
Gender of Substantives	19
Gender as indicated by Meaning	19
„ „ by Termination	19
Remarks on Gender of Substantives	20
Gender in Old Norse	21
Cases of Substantives	22
Cases in Old Norse	22
Plural of Substantives, 1st Declension	23
„ „ 2nd Declension	23
Exceptions plur. in e	24
„ plur. in er	24
Remarks on plur. of 2nd Declension	25
Plural of Substantives, 3rd Declension	25
Exceptions, plur. in er	26
„ plur. in e and er	27
Plural, 3rd Declension	27
Plural with Vowel change	28
Plural 3rd agents	28
e retained in penult.	28
e dropped in penult.	28
Plural of 4th Declension. Nouns ending in Vowel	28
„ nouns ending in el, en	29
„ „ in d, t	29
„ „ in sel, ing	29
„ „ in hed, skab, ri	29
Plural of Foreign words	30
„ Non-substantives	30

CONTENTS.

	PAGE
Plural of Proper Names	30
Singular used for Plural	30

ADJECTIVES.

Adjectives, Strong and Weak forms	32
Old Norse inflection of Adjectives	33
Adjective **liden, lille**	33
Weak form after Pronouns, Substantives, etc.	34
Gender, Adjective inflected in Neuter	34
,, Adjective not inflected in Neuter	35
Number. Plural formation, Adjectives	36
Inflection of Participle	36
Irregular Plural and Neuter forms	36
Indeclinable Adjectives	36
Comparison by Inflection	37
,, by **mere** and **mest**	38
e omitted in Comparison	38
Vowel change in Comparison	38
Irregular Comparison	38
Comparison from different root	38
Positive wanting	39
Positive and Comparative wanting	39
Non-inflected Adjectives and Participles	39
Comparative termination always e	40
Superlative termination	40
Superlative with **aller**	40

NUMERALS.

Cardinal and Ordinal Numerals	41
Multiples and Adverbs	42
Fractions	42
Sums	42
Principle of Numeration	42
Inflection of Numerals	43
Dates, Time	43

CONTENTS.

PRONOUNS.

	PAGE
Personal Pronoun 1	44
„ „ 2	44
„ „ 3	44
Remarks on the Personal Pronouns	44
Reflexive Pronouns	45
Declension of Reflexive Pronouns	45
Selv	45
Reciprocal Pronouns	46
Declension of Possessive Pronouns	46
Use of Possessive Pronouns	46
Position of	46
Declension of Demonstrative Pronouns	47
Usage of Demonstrative Pronouns	47
Examples of Demonstrative Pronouns	48
Demonstrative followed by Definite Article redundant	48
Other Demonstratives, **saa**	48
Saadan	48
Slig	49
Samme	49
Begge	49
Interrogatives declined	49
Examples of Interrogative Pronouns	50
Relatives declined	50
Usage of Relatives, **som, der, hvis, hvem**	50
Remarks on the Relatives	51
Omission of Relative	52
Examples of Relative	52
Indefinite Relatives by addition of **som, der**	53
Omission of **som, der**	54
Examples of Indefinite Relatives	54
Indefinite Pronouns, Substantive and Adjective	54
Det	55
Man	55
En	55
Nogen	55
Somme	56
Ingen	56

CONTENTS. xiii

	PAGE
Mangen	56
Anden	56
Al	57
Hver	57
Hversomhelst	57

VERBS.

	PAGE
Conjugation of Verb by Inflection	58
„ by Auxiliaries	58
Number	59
Tense	59
Moods	59
Infinitive	60
Inflexion of Infinitive	60
Participle Present	60
Participle, Past Passive	61
Voice	61
Cautions	61
Paradigm of Active Voice, at bringe	62
„ Passive at bindes	63
Interrogative Form of Verb	66
Negative form of Verb	66
Examples of various parts of the Verb	66
Være Auxiliary	69
Blive	69
Have	70
Skulle	71
Ville	71
Maatte	72
Kunne	72
Burde	73
Turde	73
Faae	73
Monne	74
Holde paa	74
Gjøre	74
Conjugations, Weak, Strong	75
1st Conjugation	75

CONTENTS.

	PAGE
List of Verbs	75
Remarks	76
2nd Conjugation	76
List of Verbs	76
Remarks	77
Vowel change	77
3rd Conjugation	78
Remarks	78
Classes under 3rd Conjugation	79
First Class, List	79
Second Class, List	80
Third Class, List	80
Fourth Class, List	81
Fifth Class, List	81
Sixth Class, List	82
Deponent Verbs	82
List	83
Reflexive Verbs	83
Reflexive Verbs, Intransitive in English	83
Reflexive, with meaning modified	84
Reflexive only	84
Impersonal Verbs with det	84
,, ,, with a subject	84
Impersonal Passive with der	84
Examples of Impersonal Verbs	85

ADVERBS.

Adverbs formed from Adjectives	86
Examples	86
Adverbs compounded with Prepositions	86
Examples	86
Adverbial Terminations	86
Participles as Adverbs	86
Pronominal Adverbs: Demonstrative	87
,, ,, Interrogative	87
,, ,, Relative	87
Comparison; by Inflection	88

CONTENTS. xv

	PAGE
Comparison by **mere, mest**	88
„ by different stem	88
Examples	88
Adverbs according to meaning:—	
Temporal	89
Examples	89
Local	90
Denoting rest at	90
Examples	90
Adverbs of Manner	91
„ of Degree	91
„ of Negation	91
„ **jo**	91

PREPOSITIONS.

	PAGE
Prepositions, government of	92
„ in composition	92
List of: **ad**	92
„ **af**	92
„ **an**	93
„ **bag**	93
„ **efter**	93
„ **for**	93
„ **fra**	93
„ **før**	94
„ **hos**	94
„ **i**	94
„ **iblandt**	94
„ **igjennem**	94
„ **imod**	94
„ **imellem**	95
„ **med**	95
„ **om**	95
„ **over**	96
„ **paa**	96
„ **til**	97
„ **trods**	98
„ **uden**	98

		PAGE
List :—under	. . . .	99
,, ved	. . . .	99

CONJUNCTIONS.

Coordinate Conjunctions :—Copulative .	. . . . .	100
,, ,, Disjunctive	. . . . .	100
,, ,, Adversative	. . . . .	100
,, ,, Causative	. . . . .	100
Subordinate :— Temporal	. . . . .	101
,, Causative	. . . . .	102
,, Conditional	. . . . .	102
,, Concessive	. . . . .	103
,, Final	. . . . .	103
,, of Comparison	. . . . .	104

INTERJECTIONS.

Exclamations	. . . .	105
Jo	. . . .	105
Dog	. . . .	105
Nok	. . . .	105
Vel	. . . .	106
Interjectional phrases	. . . .	106

CONSTRUCTION.

SYNTAX OF THE SIMPLE SENTENCE.

SUBJECT AND PREDICATE.

Idioms	. . . .	107
Concord	. . . .	107
False Concord of the Verb	. . . . . .	107
Adjective Superlative	. . . .	108
Past Participle, concord	. . . . . .	108
Adjective, concord	. . . .	108
Personal Pronouns, concord	. . . . .	109
Examples of Idiom in concord	. . . .	109

CONTENTS.

IMPERSONALS.

	PAGE
Impersonal Expressions	109
Det, der with Examples	109
Verbs, Impersonal	110
Man	110
Examples of Impersonal Expressions	111

SUBSTANTIVE.

Substantive in Apposition	112
Genitive Case	112
Other equivalents to English Genitive	113
Dative and Accusative	113
Dative with Examples	113
Dative Inflexion in Old Norse	113
Accusative with Examples	113
Substantive in definitions of measure	114
Examples of Syntax of Substantive	115

ARTICLE.

Article	116
Idioms of Indefinite Article	116
,, of Definite Article	116
Den antecedent	117
Article with **al, hel, selv**, &c.	117
Definite Article omitted	118

ADJECTIVE.

Adjective, differs from English	119
,, Concord	119
,, used substantivally	120

PRONOUN.

Idiom of Possessive Pronouns in Vocative	121
Third Person used for Second	121
Relative Pronouns, **Som**	122
Der	122

	PAGE
Hvem	122
Hvilken	122
Hvo Hvad	122
Relative omitted	122
Demonstrative used for Relative	122
Reflexive **sig, sin**	123
,, **Dem, Deres**	123

VERB.

Tenses	124
Historic Present	124
Present Tense for Future	124
Skal, use of	124
Skal, meaning of	124
Perfect for Aorist	124
Past for Present	124
Moods	125
Sign of Subjunctive omitted	125
Faar, sign of the future	125
Optative and Potential	125
Infinitive, **at**, omitted	126
Have, omitted	126
Verb of Motion omitted	126
Infinitive as Noun	126
Explicit clause with **at**	127
Participle, Present	127
,, with **blive**	127
,, Passive Absolute	128
Active Voice idiom	128
Passive reflexive	128
,, in **es**, when not used	128
,, in **es**, Aorist	129
,, inflected and by auxiliary	129

SYNTAX OF THE COMPOUND SENTENCE.

Syntax universal not discussed here	130
Idiom of the negative clause	130
Substantial clauses introduced by **at**, that	130

CONTENTS.   xix

	PAGE
Omission of **at**	130
Subordinate Clauses, Temporal	131
,, Causal	131
,, Conditional, with **if**	132
,, ,, without conjunction	132
Indicative for Subjunctive in Conditional	133
Examples of Conditional Sentences.	133
Concessive Sentences	134
Actual Concessions	134
Imaginary Concessions	134
With Particle omitted	135
Alternative Concessions	135
Final Sentences	135
Sentences denoting Consequence	136
Consequence expressed by Infinitive	136
Consequent after Negative Clause	136
Sentences implying Comparison with **som**	136
Of imaginary cases with **som om**	137
Comparative with **end**	137
Comparative of proportion **jo, desto**	137

ELLIPSE.

Ellipse of Verb of Motion	138
,, of Inceptive Verb	138
,, of Auxiliary Verb	138
,, of Substantive	139
,, of Preposition	139
,, of Conjunction	139
,, of Details of Syntax	140
,, of Article	140

PLEONASM.

Definite Article redundant	141
Pronoun	141
Preposition	141
Infinitive	141

ORDER.

	PAGE
Generally, same as in English	142
Imitation of German style	142
Differs from English	142
Position of Object in Predicate	142
,, of Object after **whosoever**	142
,, of Negative in Predicate	143
,, of Subject in Exclamations	143
Nominative after Verb, when sentence begins with non-subject	143
,, ,, in Apodosis	143
Position of Adverb, after and before Verb	144
Not can, not will, &c.	144
Examples of Negatives before Verb	144
Negative after Verb	145
Examples of Negative	145
Negative in Questions and in Protasis	146
Position of the Article	146
Alphabetical List of Phrases	147
Epistolary forms	164
Example of Norwegian spelling and pronunciation	170

I. LETTERS.

THE ALPHABET.

Character.				Name.	Sound.
𝔄	a	A	a	ah	ă in *răther, găther*.
𝔅	b	B	b	bey	b
ℭ	c	C	c	cey	s and k.
𝔇	d	D	d	dey	d
𝔈	e	E	e	ey	ĕ in *lĕt, ĕnd, thĕre*.
𝔉	f	F	f	eff	f
𝔊	g	G	g	gay	g in *get, got*, and y.
𝔥	h	H	h	haw	h
𝔍	i	I	i	ee	ee and i, *feel, fill*.
𝔍	j	J	j	yod	y in *yes*.
𝔎	k	K	k	kaw	k and ch.
𝔏	l	L	l	el	l
𝔐	m	M	m	em	m
𝔑	n	N	n	en	n
𝔒	o	O	o	o	ŏ and oo, *hope, hop, move*.
𝔓	p	P	p	pay	p
𝔔	q	Q	q	koo	koo
𝔑	r	R	r	err	r in *terrible, revenge*.
𝔖	ſs	S	s	ess	s in *suffer, slow*.
𝔗	t	T	t	tay	t and tz.
𝔘	u	U	u	u	oo in *mōod, stŏod*.
𝔙	v	V	v	vey	v in *vine*.
𝔛	x	X	x	eks	x in *sex*.
𝔜	y	Y	y	y	u in *purely*, ie in *yield*, ui iu *muir*.
𝔷	z	Z	z	set	z
𝔄𝔈	æ	Æ	æ	æ	aī in *maid, said*.
𝔒	ø	Ø	ø		i in *girl, sir*.

B

Remarks on the Alphabet.

Orthography.

The following must begin with a capital letter:
Every word that begins a sentence.

Every substantive; as en Mand, *a man*; or word used as a substantive; as en Reisende, *a traveller*; en Andens Bröd *another's bread*.

The pronouns I, Jer, *ye, your*; De, Dem, Deres, *you, your* as used instead of du, *thou*, in conversation.

The indefinite pronoun, En, *one*.

Up to late times the Gothic characters were universally used in the Dano-Norwegian language, but many books are now printed in Roman characters, which seem likely to supersede the Gothic or German.

In Swedish the Roman characters are always employed.

Pronunciation.

VOWELS.

aa aa is sounded like the English oa in coal; as
Skaal, *Good health!* (pronounced Skoal);
and sometimes like aw, in hawk. (see p. 8, line 6 infra).

e e final, when the accent is on the penultimate, or, antepenultimate, sounds like e in fodder; as
at reise til Odde, *to be going to Odde* (not Oddey).

e after a vowel is mute; as in the last syllable:
lad gaae, *let go*; Træer, *trees*.

and is now mostly omitted in the written language:
at bo, *to dwell*, for, at boe. at se, *to see*, for, at see; vi saa, for, vi saae.

ē long sounds like a in care; as
> bedre seent end aldrig (beydre saint en aldrey), *better late than never.*

ĕ short is sounded like e in set; as en Hest, *a horse.*

Except that e is pronounced like English ee in the personal pronoun De, *you*; de, *they*; and the definite article plural, de, *the*, as
> De der, *you there* (pron. Dee dare);
> de kommer snart, *they will soon be here*;
> de store Byer, *the large towns.*

ī long = ee, as ti Miil, *ten miles.*

short = i in fig, as, der ligger han, *there he lies.*

ō long has an intermediate sound between the English vowel sounds in too and toe; as
> du bor meget smukt her, *you are nicely lodged here* (pron. boor).

Sometimes ō takes the sound of aa = o in more, as in
> otte, *eight.*   ovenpaa, *up above.*

ŏ short = o in not; as
> Nok, *enough*
> Fos, *a waterfall*;
> Solen opgaar over godt og ondt, *the sun rises upon good and bad* (pron. Sōlen ŏpgōar over gŏdt ŏg oondt).

ū long, oo in brood, and short, oo in good.
> Gutten gik ud og ind i Huset, *the boy had the run of the house* (gŏŏtten yik ōod ŏg in ee Hōŏset).

ȳ long is sounded like the French u; as
> ȳdre, *outer.*   paraplȳ, *an umbrella.*

y̆ short, like o.

ǣ long = a, in hare.
> det blæser stærkt, *it blows hard* (pron. blaiser stairkt)

det kommer engelsk Arbeide meget nær (pron. nair), *it is almost as good as English workmanship*;
han blev ædru, *he was sober* (pron. aidru).

ǣ short = e in leg; as

Bordet er dækket, *the table is laid* (pron. decket);
Ægget vil lære Hønen, *the egg wants to teach the hen* (pron. egget).

æ is also used in Norwegian school-books to represent phonetically the English a, in am, had, sat, bat, happy, family; so that, Ai æm glæd hi hæs kaald æ kæb, is put to stand for, *I am glad he has called a cab*, where we should rather have expected the short a.

ø | ø long, sometimes written ö, resembles the sound of the French eu or the German ö:

Kjøreturen førte os gjennem en Skov, *the drive took us through a wood* (pron. Chiurretooren firte).

ø short, sounds like i in bird:

Maa jeg spørge, *may I ask?* (pron. spur-ge).
Tanken forfølger mig, *the idea haunts me* (pron. forfulg-er).

DIPHTHONGS.

ei ai | In ei, ai, oi, au, each letter is pronounced distinctly, but yet
oi au | so as to make one syllable.
øi | øi something like ey in eye:

fyre Øine seer meer end to, *four eyes see more than two*;
bær Tøiet ind i Værelset, *carry the luggage into the room*.

CONSONANTS.

c q | c, q, x, z, occur only in words of foreign origin, the Norse
x z | equivalents being s and k for c, k for q, ks for x.
d | d is mute before st, as bedst, *best* (pron. best), sidst, *last* (pron. sist), Pidsk, *a whip* (pron. Pisk).

Also after l and n, in which case the preceding vowel becomes short; as

Ild, *fire* (pron. ill);
Uld, *wool* (pron. ool);
Kande, *a tankard* (pron. Kanne).

Also the d is almost inaudible in many words for which no general rule can be given; as

lad gaae, (pron. la' go) sagde han, (pr. sa' han), *let go, said he.*

But d final is pronounced in some words like t; as

hid og did, *hither and thither* (pron. heet, deet).

f f is sounded like v in the preposition af, as in the corresponding English word 'of'; as fem af dem, *five of them* (pron. av).

g g is mute before j in the same syllable, gj being sounded like the English y; as gjøre, *to do* (pron. yürre).

Before n, it goes to form the sound ngn; as

Vogn, *a cart* (pron. Vongn);
Regn, *rain*, rengn; Ragnhild (pron. Rangnhild).

g is pronounced like y, before l, as

Negl, *nail* (pron. nail, as in English);
Snegl, *snail*;
Fugl, *bird* (pron. fool).

Also before i and y; as

han gik, *he went* (pron. yik).

mute after i, at the end of a word; as

daarlig, *poor, mean* (pron. doarly).

Also in the pronouns jeg, mig, dig, sig, it is softened into y, pronounced yey, mey, dey, sey.

ng = ng in *sing, singer, bell-ringer*; as

gamle Fugle ere ikke lette at fange med F ng-rene, *old birds are not easy to catch with the fingers.*

h   h is mute before **v** and **j**; as
hvad hjælper det? *what avails it?* (pron. yelper).

Also after t at the beginning of a syllable; as thi, *for* (pron. tee).

k   k is sounded hard before **n**; as
Knut, *Canute*; Kniv, *a knife*.

k in some localities is pronounced like ch in *chair*; before i, j, y and æ; as

Kirke, *church*.   Kjære, *dear*.   Kyllinger, *chickens*.

sk   sk before i and j, is pronounced like sh:
skjære, *to cut* (pron. shai-re).   Skinnet bedrager ofte, *appear-*
et Skjørt, *a petticoat* (pron. shirt).   *ances are often deceitful*;
et Skib, *a ship* (pron. ship).   (pron. shinnet).

And before e in some words; as
en Ske, *a spoon* (pron. shay).   kanske, *may be* (pron. kanshay).

sj   sj is pronounced like sh; as
sjelden, *rare* (pron. shyelden).   Sjæl, *soul* (pron. shyail).

t   t before i = tz, as Station (pron. statzion).

General Remarks.

b, g, v, are sounded like p, k, f, when t follows by inflection; as

tabt, *lost*, from tabe (pron. tapt).   have, havt, *had*.
lægge lagt, *laid*.   grov, grovt, *coarse*.
styg, stygt, *ugly*.

In verbal substantives f takes the place of v in writing; as
drive, Drift; skrive, Skrift; love, Løfte.

dt of inflected words is pronounced like tt; as
møde, mødte, mødt; god, godt; sende, sendte, sendt.

kv is now generally written instead of qv; as
Kvinde, *a woman*, instead of Qvinde.

PRONUNCIATION.

Words ending in et, or, en, preceded by a double consonant (as mm, kk), omit one of these consonants, when in the course of declension the e has been dropped; as

> gammel, *old*; nom. pl. gamle, not gammele; drukken, sing. drukne, pl. *drunk.*

If the word ends in r, both consonants are retained; as

> Vakker, *pretty*, vakkre; tapper, *brave*, tappre; Datter, *daughter*, Döttre.

e has two sounds: 1. long, like a in day; e.g.

> Sne, *snow* (pron. snay).   Ed, *an oath* (pron. aid).

2. short, like e in crest; e.g.

> Hest, *a horse.*   Dreng, *a lad.*

The same sounds, viz. ē long and ĕ short, are also expressed by the diphthong æ; as

> Præst, Gæst, hest, mæt, træt, let, slet, spænde, kjende, træffe.

Similarly the sounds of ō, ŏ, can be represented by aa, long or short, thus, in Fos, Top, Hof, Stok, the o is equivalent to aa short; in Klog, Koge, Krog, Sprog, oven, doven, Lov, Skov, sove, vove, vor, it resembles aa long.

Sometimes a vowel is doubled to express the long sound; as

> Been, *leg.*   Viin, *wine.*   Huus, *house.*

but when the Article is added, one vowel is dropped; thus

> Benet, *the leg.*   Vinen, *the wine.*   Huset, *the house.*

and conversely the consonant is doubled to show that the preceding vowel is short; as

> Gut, Gutten, *the boy.*   Seer, *I see* (also written ser).
> er De vis paa? adj. *are you sure!*   en Viis, *a wise man*, subs.

But always

> Een, *one*, to distinguish it from the Art. en, *a*, or *an*;

A few examples of the phonetic rendering of English words in Norwegian manuals, may serve to illustrate the pronunciation.

English.	Norse spelling to represent the English sounds.
Law.	laa.
Broad road.	braad raad.
Promise.	praammis.
A load.	a laad.
I may.	ei me.
I must.	ei möst.
Cold salt water.	kaald saalt uaater.
I know. I knew.	ei naa. ei nju.
I have known.	ei hæv naan.
I buy. I bought.	ei bei. ei baat.
I have bought a boat.	ei hæv baat æ baat.
Glove.	gløv.
Hair.	hær.
Razor.	ræser.
To use.	tu juus.
Mountain.	mauntin.
Crowd.	Kraud.
Shoemaker.	Sjumeeker.
To attack.	tu ættæk.
Common.	kaammøn.
Arable land.	aræble lænd.
Part.	part.
To dance.	tu dæns.
News.	njuus.
Barley.	barli.
Carry.	kærri.
Now I will just tell you what you shall do.	Nau ei uill dsjøst tell ju huaatt ju sjæll du.

II. WORDS.

ACCIDENCE.

The PARTS OF SPEECH may be most conveniently classified as follows:—

1. Articles.
2. Substantives.
3. Adjectives.
4. Numerals.
5. Pronouns.
6. Verbs.
7. Adverbs.
8. Prepositions.
9. Conjunctions.
10. Interjections.

NUMBER. There are two numbers in Danish and Norse, the Singular and the Plural; as

S. Mand, *man*.
Hest, *horse*.
By, *town*.
Pl. Mænd, *men*.
Heste, *horses*.
Byer, *towns*.

CASE. The Genitive in both numbers ends in s; as

Eriks Hund, *Eric's dog*;
gode Venners Raad, *good friends' advice*.

GENDER. There are two genders, the Common, and the Neuter; as

C. en Mand, *a man*.
en Kone, *a woman*.
N. et Barn, *a child*.
et Træ, *a tree*.

INFLECTION in the Norse language proceeds by two methods; viz. by change of termination, as By, Bys, Byer; or, by change of the stem vowel; as

han drikker, *he drinks*;   han drak, *he drank*.

Such change of vowel is either by MUTATION (Omlyd), or by GRADATION (Aflyd).

MUTATION takes place both in the Inflection of words, and in the Formation of words by derivation. On this principle the vowel sounds a, aa, regularly become æ, as in Mand, mænd; Navn, nævne; Taa, *a toe*, Tæer, *toes.* o becomes ø; as Bog, *book,* Bøger, *books.* u becomes y; as ud, *out,* ydre, *outer.*

> *Obs.* In one single word a becomes ø,; viz. Barn, Børn. Døttre is from the old form of the sing. Dotter.
>
> o sometimes becomes y in derivation; as
>
> ost, *cheese*;   at yste, *to make cheese.*

GRADATION (Aflyd) is the vowel change which takes place in the Inflection of Strong Verbs, and words derived from them:

> jeg strider, *I strive.*   jeg tager, *I take.*
> vi strede, *we strove.*   jeg tog, *I took.*

ARTICLES.

There are two kinds of Article, the Indefinite en et *a* or *an*; and the Definite, en, *the*, suffixed to Substantives, and den, det, plural de, prefixed to Adjectives.

INDEFINITE. The Indef. Art. is used only in the Singular number, en for the common gender; and et for the Neuter; as

    en Mand, *a man.*   en Hund, *a dog.*
    Mænd, *men.*   Hunde, *dogs,*
    et Æble, *an apple.*   en gammel Stol, *an old chair.*
    Æbler, *apples.*   et høit Træ, *a tall tree.*

DEFINITE. The form and position of the Def. Art. varies according as it is used with a Substantive or an Adjective.

With Substantives, the Def. Art. is used as a suffix; being in the Sing. number for the common gender, en or n, for the neuter et or t. In the plural for both genders it is ene or ne; thus:

   c. Manden, *the man.*   c. Kongen, *the king.*
     Mandens, *the man's.*   Kongens, *the king's.*
     Mændene, *the men.*   Kongerne, *the kings.*
     Mændenes, *the mens'.*   Kongernes, *the kings'.*
   n. Barnet, *the child.*   n. Æblet, *the apple.*
     Barnets, *the childs'.*   Æblets, *the apple's.*
     Børnene, *the children.*   Æblerne, *the apples.*
     Børnenes, *the childrens'.*   Æblernes, *the apples'.*

With Adjectives, the Def. Art. is, in the sing. number for the common gender den, for the neuter det. In the plural for both genders it is de.

The Adjective following the Def. Art. always takes the termination e; thus:

den store Hund, *the large dog*.	det høie Træ, *the tall tree*.
den store Hunds, *the large dog's*.	det høie Træs, *the tall tree's*.
de store Hunde, *the large dogs*.	de høie Træer, *the tall trees*.
de store Hundes, *of the large dogs*.	de høie Træers, *of the tall trees*.

The form of an Adjective following the Indefinite Article is not affected by it.

Remarks on the Articles.

The Def. Art. is **en, et, ene**, when the Substantive to which it is suffixed does not end in **e**; when it does end in **e**, the Def. Art. is represented by **n, t, ne**.

Neuter substantives ending in **el**, omit the **e** which precedes l when the Def. Art. is suffixed; as

Middel, Middlet, *the means*;
Tempel, Templet, *the temple*;
Æsel, Æslet, *the ass*.

But those of the common gender retain the **e** before l; as

Himmel, Himmelen, *the sky*;
Engel, Engelen, *the angel*;
Regel, Regelen, *the rule*.

Substantives that end in **er**, and retain the **e** before **r** in the Plural, lose the Plural **e**; as

Bageren, *the baker*,   Bagerne, *the bakers*, not Bagerene.

But those that sink the **e** precedent, retain the plural **e**; as

Fingeren, Fingrene, *the fingers*.

In some Substantives the consonant is doubled before the Def. Art.; as

Gut, gutten, *the boy*.   Lam, lammet, *the lamb*.

Et Øie, *an eye*, makes plur. nom. Øine, *eyes*; gen. Øines, *of eyes*. Definite Øiet, Øiets; pl. Øinene, Øinenes.

Et Øre, *an ear*; pl. Øren, or Ører; genit. Ørens, Ørers; Def. Ørerne, Ørene, genit. Ørernes, Ørenes.

En Oxe, *an ox*, pl. Oxer; Def. Oxerne, rarely Oxnene.

Et Menneske, *a human being*; pl. Mennesker; Def. Mennesket, Menneskene.

Verbum, *a verb*, makes Verbet, Verbene.

> *Obs.* In ordinary conversation the r of the plural termination is dropped before the definite art.; as Guttene, *for* gutterne, *the boys*.
> except where no audible e precedes the r, as Trærne, *the trees*.
> So also the t of the neuter is slurred over, Huset, *the house* being pronounced Huse.

The Indef. Art. is properly the numeral een, *one*, neut. eet, without the accent.

The Def. Art. suffixed comes from the demonstrative pronoun hin. In Old Norse hin is similarly appended to Substantives as an Article, but both Subs. and Art. are inflected; e.g.

N. Konungr-inn   G. Konungs-ins.
    Land-it   Lands-ins.
    Hjarta-t   Hjarta-ns.

This will explain such forms as

Landsens, *of the land*;
Havsens bund, *the bottom of the sea*;
Livsens Træ, *the tree of life*,
Hjertens Grund, *the bottom of the heart*;
Husens Folk, *they of the household*;
Menneskens Søn, *the Son of Man*.

Al, *all*, selv, *self*, begge, *both*, cannot take the Def. Art. of the Adj. before them: we must say,

al Maden, *all the food*;
selv Herren, *the gentleman himself*;
begge Brødrene, *both the brothers*.

With hel, *whole*, halv, *half*, either form of the Def. Art. may be used; as

>hele Dagen, or den hele Dag, *the whole day*;
>halve Riget, or det halve Rige, *half the kingdom*;
>forrige Dagen, *the day previous*; but, den 4do i forrige Maaned, *the 4th ultimo*.

Sometimes both forms of the Definite Art. are used at once; as

>den store Bjældebukken, *the big bell-goat*;
>den dybe Kulpen, *the deep pool*.

Den, det, de, being of the nature of a Pronoun, must be used and not the suffix, as the antecedent to a following Relative; as

>den Mand som sagde mig, *the man who told me* (not Manden);
>den Fornøielse at dandse med Dem, *the pleasure of dancing with you* (not Fornøielsen at).

Examples.

The following examples will serve to familiarise the reader with the forms of the Article.

>Gud bevare Kongen, *God save the King*.
>Koen døer mens Græsset groer, *while the grass grows the cow dies*.
>sælg ikke Bjørnens Hud før Du har fanget den, *sell not the bear's skin before you have caught the bear*.
>det stille Vand har den dybe Grund, *still waters run deep*.
>Dovenskab er Djævelens Hovedpude, *laziness is the devil's pillow*.
>hvor Aadslet er der skulle Ornene forsamles, *where the carcass is there will the eagles be gathered together*.
>et Ord er et Ord og en Mand en Mand, *an honest man's word is as good as his bond*.
>om Natten ere alle Katte graa, *all cats are grey in the dark*.
>mange Bække smaa gjør en stor Aa, *many a little makes a mickle*.
>jeg gav ham et bestemt Afslag, *I gave him a flat refusal*.
>han bander som en Tyrk, *he swears like a trooper*.

SUBSTANTIVE. 15

blinde Høne kan ogsaa finde et Korn, *even blind hens can find a grain of corn.*
vi maa bruge Apostelenes Kjøretøi, *we must ride on Shanks's mare.*
det er en bidende Kulde, *it is bitterly cold.*
en lille Bitte Mand, *a little bit of a man.*
Taarerne kom hende i Øinene, *the tears came into her eyes.*
han puffer sig frem med Albuerne, *he pushes his way out with his elbows.*
det bestøvlede Kat, *puss in boots.*
den hele Dag, *the whole day.*
en heel Dag, *a whole day.*
hele Dagen, *all the day.*
hele den Dag, *for the whole of that day.*
den ulykkelige Ingeborgs Mand, *the unfortunate Ingeborg's husband.*
han skulde være Kong over det hele Land, *he was to be king over the whole land.*
de behøvede en heel Dag at gaae, før de kom til Bjergene, hvor de sorte Skove voxte lige op mod Himlen. *They had to walk a whole day before they came to the mountains where the dark woods grew far up towards the sky.*
vi ere Luftens Døttre, svarede de Andre, vi sprede Blomsternes Duft gjennem Luften, og sende Vederquægelse og Lægedom. Naar vi i tre hundrede Aar have stræbt at gjøre det Gode vi kunne, da faae vi en udødelig Sjæl, og tage Deel i Menneskenes evige Lykke. *We are daughters of the air, answered the others, we waft the flowers' fragrance through the air, and send refreshment and healing. When we have striven for three hundred years to do all the good we can, we receive an immortal soul, and share in the eternal happiness of mankind.*
Du stakkels lille Havfrue har stræbt efter det Samme som vi, Du har lidt og taalt, hævet Dig til Luftaandernes Verden, nu kan Du selv gjennem gode Gjerninger skabe Dig en udødelig Sjæl. *You poor little Mermaid, you have striven after the same as we, you have suffered and endured, and raised yourself up to the world of aërial spirits, and now you too by good deeds can gain for yourself an immortal soul.*

NOUNS SUBSTANTIVE.

GENDER. The gender of Substantives is either Common or Neuter; and is defined, in the Singular, by means of the Article, en, or den, for the common, et or det for the neuter.

CASE. There are two cases of Substantives distinguished by inflection, viz. the Nominative, and the Genitive, which latter always ends in s.

NUMBER. There are two numbers, the Singular and Plural: the latter, when the termination varies from that of the Sing., ends in e, or r.

Declension.

Hence arise two Classes, making four Declensions:
1. The Simple, containing all nouns ending in e unaccented.
2. The Complex, comprehending all others.

In the First Declension, the Plural is formed by adding r.
,, Second ,, the Plural is the same as the Singular.
,, Third ,, the Plural is formed by adding e.
,, Fourth ,, the Plural is formed by adding er.

PARADIGM OF FIRST, OR SIMPLE DECLENSION.

INDEFINITE.

Common Gender.

Sing. N. en Kjæmpe, *a warrior.*   Plur. Kjæmper, *warriors.*
G. en Kjæmpes, *a warrior's.*   Kjæmpers, *warriors'.*

N. en Pige, *a girl.*   Piger, *girls.*
G. en Piges, *a girl's.*   Pigers, *girls'.*

DECLENSION. 17

Neuter Gender.

Sing. N. et Stykke, *a piece.*   Plur. Stykker, *pieces.*
G. et Stykkes, *a piece's.*   Stykkers, *pieces'.*

DEFINITE.

Common Gender.

Sing. N. Kjæmpen, *the warrior.*   Plur. Kjæmperne, *the warriors.*
G. Kjæmpens, *the warrior's.*   Kjæmpernes, *the warriors'.*

N. Pigen, *the girl.*   Pigerne, *the girls.*
G. Pigens, *the girl's.*   Pigernes, *the girls'.*

PARADIGM OF SECOND DECLENSION.

INDEFINITE.

Sing. N. et Ror, *a rudder.*   Plur. Ror, *rudders.*
G. et Rors, *a rudder's.*   Rors, *rudders'.*

DEFINITE.

Sing. N. Roret, *the rudder.*   Plur. Rorene, *the rudders.*
G. Rorets, *the rudder's.*   Rorenes, *the rudders'.*

PARADIGM OF THE THIRD DECLENSION.

INDEFINITE.

Sing. N. en Hest, *a horse.*   Plur. Heste, *horses.*
G. en Hests, *a horse's.*   Hestes, *horses'.*

DEFINITE.

Sing. N. Hesten, *the horse.*   Plur. Hestene, *the horses.*
G. Hestens, *the horse's.*   Hestenes, *the horses'.*

PARADIGM OF THE FOURTH DECLENSION.

INDEFINITE.

Sing. N. en Sag, *a thing.*   Plur. Sager, *things.*
G. en Sags, *a thing's.*   Sagers, *things'.*

DEFINITE.

Sing. N. Sagen, *the thing*   Plur. Sagerne, *the things.*
G. Sagens, *the thing's.*   Sagernes, *of the things.*

C

In every declension nouns occur which change the root vowel in the plural, either by Mutation (Omlyd), or by Gradation (Aflyd).

The following is a list of words of this kind in common use.

First Declension.

Sing.	Plur.
en Bonde, *a farmer.*	Bønder, *farmers.*

Second Declension.

Sing.	Plur.
en Gaas, *a goose.*	Gæs, *geese.*
en Mand, *a man.*	Mænd, *men.*
et Barn, *a child.*	Børn, *children.*

Third Declension.

Sing.	Plur.
en Fader, *a father.*	Fædre, *fathers.*
en Broder, *a brother.*	Brødre, *brothers.*
en Moder, *a mother.*	Mødre, *mothers.*
en Datter, *a daughter.*	Døttre, *daughters.*

Fourth Declension.

Sing.	Plur.	Sing.	Plur.
en And, *a duck.*	Ænder.	en Rod, *a root.*	Rødder.
en Stand, *an estate.*	Stænder.	en Tang, *tongs.*	Tænger.
en Stang, *a pole.*	Stænger.	en Taa, *a toe.*	Tæer.
en So, *a sow.*	Søer.	en Bog, *a book.*	Bøger.
en Nat, *a night.*	Nætter.	en Haand, *a hand.*	Hænder.
en Bod, *a shop.*	Bøder.	en Klo, *a claw.*	Kløer.
en Glod, *live coal.*	Gløder.	en Rand, *rim.*	Rænder.
en Not, *a net.*	Nøter.	en Tand, *tooth.*	Tænder.
en Kraft, *strength.*	Kræfter.	en Ko, *a cow.*	Køer.
en Fod, *a foot.*	Fødder.		

GENDER.

THE GENDERS OF NOUNS in the Norse language must be learnt by observation, as they cannot be comprehended under any general rules. The following classification will, however, be a guide in many cases.

Gender as indicated by MEANING :—
1. Common Gender.
    Names of living beings, as, en Mand; of plants individually, Birken, *the birch*.
    Of heavenly bodies, as, Solen, *the sun*.
2. Neuter Gender.
    Material, as, Guldet, *the gold*.
    Collective nouns, as, Folket, *the people*; Græsset, *the grass*.
    Names of towns and countries, as, det sydlige Norge, *Southern Norway*.
    Names of languages, as, De taler godt Norsk, *you speak good Norse*.

Exceptions. Living things.

et Fruentimmer, *a woman*; et Menneske, *a human being*; et Æsel, *an ass*; et Dyr, *a beast*; et Svin, *a pig*; et Lam, *a lamb*; et Kid, *a kid*; et Barn, *a child*.

Material.

Stenen, *stone*; Melk, The, Kaffe, which are common.

GENDER indicated by TERMINATION :—
1. Common Gender.
    Nouns ending in e, de, t, st, ste, er, en, else, sel, ing, ske, dom, hed.
2. Neuter.
    Nouns ending in eri, ende, dømme, maal, skab.

Exceptions.

et Rige, *a kingdom*; **et** Ærme, *a sleeve*; **et** Ønske, *a wish*.
et Skridt, *a step*; **et** Værelse, *a chamber*; **et** Bidsel, *a bridle*, are neuter.

Kundskab, *knowledge*; Troskab, *faithfulness*, and many other abstract substantives, are of the common gender.

Remarks on Gender.

1. Some names of places with a termination implying Common gender take the neuter article before them, and the common at the end; as

    det frugtbare Hedemarken, *the fertile Hedemark.*

Compound nouns follow the gender of the last part; as

   Snehætten, Romsdalshornet, en Landsmand, *a countryman*, et Armbaand, *a bracelet*, en Vildkat, *a wild-cat*, et Vildsvin, *a wild-boar*.

Exceptions.

en Tid, *a time*.   **et** Maaltid, *a meal*.
en Stav, *a staff*.   **et** Bogstav, *a letter*.

2. Names of Languages, when the def. art. is suffixed to them, are treated as common; e. g.

   Græsken og Latinen ere udsprungne of samme Rod, *Greek and Latin are sprung from the same root.*

3. Non-substantives used as substantives are neuter; e. g.

   Mit Ja er Saa godt som **Dit** Nei, *My yes is as good as your no.*

4. Some words take a different gender, according to difference in their meaning; as

   et Thing, *a parliament*; **en** Ting, *a thing*; **en** Raad, *a councillor*; **et** Raad, *advice*.

GENDER.

Some words are **neuter** in Danish, and **common** in Norwegian; as

DANISH.	NORWEGIAN.	DANISH.	NORWEGIAN.
Sandet, *sand*.	Sanden.	et Møl, *moth*.	en Møl.
et Mos, *moss*.	en Mos.	et Helbred, *health*.	en Helbred.
et Ved, *firewood*.	en Ved.	et Kys, *a kiss*.	en Kys.

but conversely,

en Rus, *drunkenness*.	et Rus.	en Kind, *cheek*.	et Kind.
en Skal, *rind*.	et Skal.	en Regn, *rain*.	et Regn.
en Trold, *goblin*.	et Trold.	en Rede, *a nest*.	et Rede.

5. Sted, *a place*, now neuter, was anciently masculine; hence arise the variants:—

isteden, istedet, *instead*; nogensteds, nogetsteds, *somewhere*; ingensteds, intetsteds, *nowhere*.

Obs. The old Norse has three genders, masc. fem. and neut. The two first primarily denoted living beings, according to sex: and the neuter inanimate things: but the masc. and fem. are also used of things, and conversely the neuter is sometimes applied to living creatures, when the noun comprises both the natural genders.

The three genders are still used in the language of the country people, e. g.

masc. ein Mann, *a man*; ein Stol, *a chair*; fem. ei Kona, *a woman*; ei Dør, *a door*; neut. eit Barn, *a child*; eit Hus, *a house*.

And the same distinction of gender is observed in the language of the people even in the towns, e. g.

en Mann, en Stol, e Kone, e Dør.

Generally however the masc. and fem. are merged in the common, and we say

en Mand, en Stol, en Kone, en Dør.

CASE.

Persons and things indicated by a double appellation add the s of the genitive to the last word only; as

    Kong Olafs Hær, *King Olaf's army.*

When a proper name ends in s, an apostrophe is added between this s and the s of the genitive; e. g.

    Valders's afsides liggende Fjelddale, *the lateral valleys of Valders.*

It will be found that in Norse the inflected genitive is used commonly where in English we use the genitive with of, although the corresponding genitive form by af is also used; e. g.

    Kongen af Norge, Norges Konge, *the King of Norway.*

The preposition is omitted after nouns of measure and the like; e. g.

    et Glas Øl, *a glass of ale*; en Lap Papir, *a scrap of paper.*

Some foreign proper names, especially biblical names, retain their own form of the genitive; as

    Petri Brev, *the Epistle of Peter.*

The Old Norse had also a dative and an accusative case. Traces of the old inflection still remain in certain phrases; as

    i Tide, *in time*; i Live, *alive*; at komme til Live igjen, *to come to life again*;
    at falde til Fode, *to submit.*
    til Fods, *on foot*; til Havs, *to sea*; to til Mands, *two each.*
    ad aare, *till next year.*
    gaac en til Haande, *to help one.*
    komme En til Hænde, *to come to hand.*

Sometimes the preposition and substantive are written as one word, and used adverbially; as

    at gaae tilgrunde, *to sink to the bottom, be ruined.*
    komme tilsyne, *to come to light.*   tilsengs, *to bed.*
    at gaae tilværks, *to set about.*   nutildags, *nowadays.*

NUMBER.

On the Formation of the Plural of Nouns.

First Declension.

The plural ends in **r** of all words that in the singular end in **e** unaccented; as

en Abe, *an ape,* Aber, *apes.*
et Æble, *an apple,* Æbler, *apples.*

Some, moreover, **change the stem-vowel** by Omlyd :—

Bonde, *a peasant,* plur. Bønder.
Oxe, *an ox,* makes both Oxer, and Øxen, Øxne.
Øre, *an ear,*   ,,   ,, Ører   ,, Øren.
Øie, *an eye,*   ,,   ,, Øine   ,, Øien.

Second Declension.

The following take **no additional termination** for the plural.

Most neuters ending in a consonant; as

	Sing.	Plur.	Sing.	Plur.
et	Ax, *an ear of corn.*	Ax.	Stød, *push.*	Stød.
	Aar, *a year.*	Aar.	Skud, *a shot.*	Skud.
	Baal, *funeral fire.*	Baal.	Slag, *stroke.*	Slag.
	Brød, *a loaf of bread.*	Brød.	Svar, *answer.*	Svar.
	Lam, *a lamb.*	Lam.	Tab, *loss.*	Tab.
	Lys, *light.*	Lys.	Forsøg, *attempt.*	Forsøg.
	Svin, *swine.*	Svin.	Forhør, *examination.*	Forhør.
	Æg, *egg.*	Æg.	Forbund, *alliance.*	Forbund.
	Brud, *fracture.*	Brud.	Paafund, *device.*	Paafund.
	Bud, *command.*	Bud.	Jordskjælv, *earth-*	Jordskjælv.
	Brøl, *roar.*	Brøl.	*quake.*	
	Hop, *jump.*	Hop.	Tillæg, *addition.*	Tillæg.
	Hyl, *howl.*	Hyl.	Greb, *grasp.*	Greb.
	Kast, *throw.*	Kast.	Sæt, *set, suit.*	Sæt.
	Spring, *leap.*	Spring.		

But

Sing.	Plur.	Sing.	Plur.
Begreb, *idea*.	Begreber.	Barn, *child*.	Børn.
Forsæt, *purpose*.	Forsætter.		

Some nouns also of the common gender ending in a consonant **add no termination** for the plural; as

en Mus, *mouse*.	Mus.	Sild, *herring*.	Sild.
Alen, *ell*.	Alen.	Tvivl, *doubt*.	Tvivl.
Feil, *fault*.	Feil.	Ting, *thing*.	Ting.

Exceptions.

The following neuters ending in a consonant **add e** for the plural.

et Bjerg, *mountain*.	Bjerge.	Skib, *ship*.	Skibe.
Blad, *leaf*.	Blade.	Sogn, *parish*.	Sogne.
Bord, *table*.	Borde.	Sund, *channel*.	Sunde.
Fad, *dish, cask*.	Fade.	Sværd, *sword*.	Sværde (Nor.).
Fjeld, *mountain*.	Fjelde.	Tag, *roof*.	Tage.
Gulv, *floor*.	Gulve.	Taarn, *tower*.	Taarne.
Hav, *sea*.	Have.	Telt, *tent*.	Telte.
Hus, *house*.	Huse.	Torv, *market*.	Torve.
Land, *land*.	Lande.	Trold, *goblin*.	Trolde.
Navn, *name*.	Navne.	Trug, *trough*.	Truge.
Skab, *cup-board*.	Skabe.	Vand, *lake*.	Vande.

The following **add er** for the plural:—

et Bryst, *breast*.	Bryster.	Skjød, *flap*.	Skjøder.
Gods, *goods*.	Godser.	Skjørt, *petticoat*.	Skjørter.
Hul, *hole*.	Huler.	Bryllup, *wedding*.	Bryllupper.
Kind, *cheek*.	Kinder.	Hoved, *head*.	Hoveder.
Lem, *limb*.	Lemmer.	Herred, *district*.	Herreder.
Lod, *weight*.	Lodder.	Marked, *fair*.	Markeder.
Loft, *loft*.	Lofter.	Bidsel, *bridle*.	Bidsler.
Sted, *place*.	Steder.	Redskab, *implement*.	Redskaber.

Obs. The forms in use in ordinary conversation are:

    Huser and Hus, *houses*.   Gulver and Gulv, *floors*.

Sometimes words which have the plural in **er** in the written language, in conversation follow the general rule; as

Hul, *holes*; Kind, *cheeks*, for Huler, Kinder.

The common people also say Mænner, *men*; Gjæsser, *geese*.

Also, in common conversation, the Norwegians make almost all nouns of the common gender which end in a consonant, end in **er** in the plural; e. g.

Hester, *horses*; Griser, *pigs*; Krister, *sprigs*.

Some people have also begun to adopt this practice in writing.

To sum up the case of neuters **ending in a consonant**:—

No additional termination is the general rule;
e is added in the written language;
er in the spoken language.

Third Declension.

The following **add e** to form the plural:—

1. Monosyllables of the common gender that end in a consonant; as

Sing.	Plur.	Sing.	Plur.
en Fisk, *a fish*.	Fiske.	Svamp, *sponge*.	Svampe.
Arm, *arm*.	Arme.	Stald, *stable*.	Stalde.
Orm, *worm*.	Orme.	Vold, *rampart*.	Volde.
Svend, *swain*.	Svende.	Elv, *river*.	Elve.
Hund, *dog*.	Hunde.	Ulv, *wolf*.	Ulve.
Gjenstand, *object*.	Gjenstande.	Gaard, *farm-stead*.	Gaarde.
Torn, *thorn*.	Torne.	Fjord, *sea-inlet*.	Fjorde.
Bjørn, *bear*.	Bjørne.	Hjort, *red-deer*.	Hjorte.
Gang, *walk*.	Gange.	Harv, *harrow*.	Harve.
Dreng, *boy*.	Drenge.	Spurv, *sparrow*.	Spurve.
Bænk, *bench*.	Bænke.	Dværg, *dwarf*.	Dværge.
Dunk, *jar*.	Dunke.	Borg, *castle*.	Borge.
Kamp, *fight*.	Kampe.	Birk, *birch-tree*.	Birke.

Sing.	Plur.	Sing.	Plur.
Stork, *stork*.	Storke.	Mur, *wall*.	Mure.
Negl, *nail*.	Negle.	Dør, *door*.	Døre.
Fugl, *bird*.	Fugle.	Gren, *branch*.	Grene.
Egn, *region*.	Egne.	Gris, *pig*.	Grise.
Vogn, *carriage*.	Vogne.	Baad, *boat*.	Baade.
Havn, *harbour*.	Havne.	Stud, *bullock*.	Stude.
Ovn, *oven*.	Ovne.	Dag, *day*.	Dage.
Hest, *horse*.	Heste.	Dug, *cloth*.	Duge.
Ost, *cheese*.	Oste.	Grav, *pit*.	Grave.
Dal, *dale*.	Dale.	Kniv, *knife*.	Knive.
Pil, *arrow*.	Pile.	Skov, *wood*.	Skove.

Words with a short vowel in the stem **double** the **consonant** in the plural.

Træl, *serf*.	Trælle.	Stok, *stick*.	Stokke.
Nar, *fool*.	Narre.	Top, *top, summit*.	Toppe.
Hat, *hat*.	Hatte.		

Exceptions.

The following **add er** for the plural:—

en Alf, *a fairy*.	Alfer.	Knop, *bud*.	Knopper.
Art, *sort*.	Arter.	Kop, *cup*.	Kopper.
Aand, *spirit*.	Aander.	Lap, *scrap*.	Lapper.
Bred, *border*.	Bredder.	Last, *vice*.	Laster.
Bøn, *prayer*.	Bønner.	Lem, *limb*.	Lemmer.
Ed, *oath*.	Eder.	Lod, *lot*.	Lodder.
Flæk (Nor.), *speck*.	Flækker.	Lok, *curl*.	Lokker.
Gjed, *she-goat*.	Gjeder.	Lyst, *pleasure*.	Lyster.
Gjæst, *guest*.	Gjæster.	Læst, *shoe-last*.	Læster.
Gran, *spruce-fir*.	Graner.	Mark, *field*.	Marker.
Gnist, *spark*.	Gnister.	Mast, *ship-mast*.	Master.
Gud, *god*.	Guder.	Myr, *marsh*.	Myrer.
Hal, *saloon*.	Haller.	Od, *point*.	Odder.
Hud, *skin*.	Huder.	Pjalt, *rag*.	Pjalter.
Kant, *edge*.	Kanter.	Prik, *dot*.	Prikker.
Klump, *lump*.	Klumper.	Rad, *rank*.	Rader.
Knap, *button*.	Knapper.	Ret, *right*.	Retter.

NUMBER.

Sing.	Plur.	Sing.	Plur.
Sag, *thing*.	Sager.	Søn, *son*.	Sønner.
Skal, *shell*.	Skaller.	Tid, *time*.	Tider.
Slump, *lot, chance*.	Slumper.	Tomt, *site*.	Tomter.
Spaan, *a chip*.	Spaaner.	Tot, *tuft*.	Totter.
Streg, *streak*.	Streger.	Urt, *herb*.	Urter.
Stump, *fragment*.	Stumper.	Ven, *friend*.	Venner.
Stund, *time, hour*.	Stunder.	Bog, *a book*.	Bøger.
Synd, *sin*.	Synder.	Æt, *origin*.	Ætter.
Sæd, *manners*.	Sæder.		

And especially words of foreign origin; as

Dunst, *vapour*.	Dunster.	Plet, *a speck*.	Pletter.
Form, *shape*.	Former.	Pris, *price*.	Priser.
Frugt, *fruit*.	Frugter.	Præst, *priest*.	Præster.
Kork, *cork*.	Korker.	Provst, *provost*.	Provster.
Plan, *a plain*.	Planer.	Bisp, *bishop*.	Bisper.

and provincial-dialect words; as

But, *tub*.	Butter.	Gut, *boy* (Norse).	Gutter.
Døl, *dalesman* (Norse).	Døler.	Lev, *loaf* (Norse).	Lever.
Fant, *gipsy* (Norse).	Fanter.	Ur, *talus of loose stones*.	Urer.
Flis, *splinter*.	Fliser.		

Some words have **both e** and **er** for the plural, the Norwegian authors preferring **er**; as

Sump, *swamp*.	Sumpe and	Sumper.
Skjelm, *pod*.	Skjelme ,,	Skjelmer.
Dunk, *jar*.	Dunke ,,	Dunker.
Skaal, *bowl*.	Skaale ,,	Skaaler.
Stav, *stick*.	Stave ,,	Staver.
Aas, *ridge*.	Aase ,,	Aaser.
Brod, *sting*.	Brodde ,,	Brodder.
Fos, *waterfall*.	Fosse ,,	Fosser.
Rem, *strap*.	Remme ,,	Remmer.

2. Substantives **in om**, as Sygdom, *sickness*, and substantives **in er**, both common and neuter, make the plural **in e**; as

Sanger, *singer*.	Sangere.	Fjeder, *feather*.	Fjedre.
Borger, *citizen*.	Borgere.	Bæger, *goblet*.	Bægere.

except Fruentimmer; pl. flere Fruentimmer, *many women*.

The following **change** the **stem-vowel** as well:—

Sing.	Plur.	Sing.	Plur.
Fader, *a father*.	Fædre.	Broder, *brother*.	Brødre.
Moder, *mother*.	Mødre.	Datter, *daughter*.	Døttre.

Obs. When the singular ends in **el, en, er**, this **e** is generally omitted in the plural. But

Substantives in **er** derived from verbs, and indicating agents, and some foreign words, **retain the e** before **r** in the plural; as

en Bager, *a baker*.	Bagere.	Keiser, *emperor*.	Keisere.
Fisker, *fisherman*.	Fiskere.	Mester, *master*.	Mestere.
Ener, *unit*.	Enere.	Kunstner, *artist*.	Kunstnere.
Græker, *Greek*.	Grækere.		

Also, most neuters **retain the e** before **r** in plural; as

Alter, *altar*.	Altere.	Kobber, *copper*.	Kobbere.
Bæger, *cup*.	Bægere.	Pulver, *powder*.	Pulvere.
Kammer, *chamber*.	Kammere.		

The following **drop the e** before **r**:—

Ager, *field*.	Agre.	Søster, *sister*.	Søstre.
Finger, *finger*.	Fingre.	Theater, *theatre*.	Theatre.
Vinter, *winter*.	Vintre.	Kloster, *abbey*.	Klostre.
Fjeder, *feather*.	Fjedre.		

Fourth Declension.

The following **add er** to form the plural:—

1. All substantives that **end in an accented** vowel; as

Aa, *rivulet*.	Aaer.	Hei, *mountain ridge*.	Heier.
Ske, *spoon*.	Skeer.		
Bro, *bridge*.	Broer.	Bo, *furniture*.	Boer.
By, *town*.	Byer.	Træ, *tree*.	Træer.
Sø, *lake*.	Søer.	Tøi, *baggage*.	Tøier.

Except

en Vei, *a road*.	Veie.	en Sko, *shoe*.	Sko, and Skoe.
en Fløi, *vane*.	Fløie.	et Knæ, *knee*.	Knæer, and Knæ.
en Høi, *hill*.	Høie.		

NUMBER.

Words ending in **el** and **en**, **add er** in the plural; as

Sing.	Plur.	Sing.	Plur.
en Kjedel, *a kettle*.	Kjedler.	et Kjøkken, *kitchen*.	Kjøkkener.
et Æsel, *ass*.	Æsler.	en Kjortel, *coat* (obsolete).	Kjortler.
en Aften, *evening*.	Aftener.	et Nøgel, *ball of thread*.	Nøgler.

Except

Engel, *an angel*.	Engle.	Himmel, *sky*.	Himmele.
Djævel, *devil*.	Djævle.	Vaaben, *weapon*.	Vaaben.

Abstract substantives in **en** have no plural; as Skrigen, *a screaming*.

Derivatives ending in **d, t, add er** in the plural; as

Drift, *impulse*.	Drifter.	Indsigt, *insight*.	Indsigter.
Væxt, *plant*.	Væxter.	Bygd, *district*.	Bygder.
Last, *weight*.	Laster.	Dyd, *virtue*.	Dyder.
Bugt, *bight, bay*.	Bugter.	Blomst, *flower*.	Blomster.
Magt, *might*.	Magter.	Kunst, *art*.	Kunster.
Slægt, *lineage*.	Slægter.		

Words ending in **sel, ing, add er** in the plural; as

Længsel, *longing*.	Længsler.	Bygning, *building*.	Bygninger.
Fængsel, *prison*.	Fængsler.	Dronning, *queen*.	Dronninger.
Hvælving, *arch*.	Hvælvinger.	Arving, *heir*.	Arvinger.

Except

Olding, *old man*.	Oldinge.	Sletning, *relation*.	Sletninge.

Words ending in **hed, skab, ri, ig, ik, ed, add er** in the plural; as

Dumhed, *stupidity*.	Dumheder.
Venskab, *friendship*.	Venskaber.
Tyveri, *theft*.	Tyverier.
Værdi, *value*.	Værdier.
Bolig, *abode*.	Boliger.
Maddik, *maggot*.	Maddiker.
Nellik, *gilliflower*.	Nelliker.
Foged, *sheriff*.	Fogeder.
Fælled, *common*.	Fælleder.

Most foreign words in use in the language make the plural in **er**—as Sofa, *a sofa*, Sofaer; Nation, *a nation*, Nationer; Verbum, *verb*, Verber.

Except those ending in **er in the singular**.

Obs. Some foreign words of the neuter gender, viz. monosyllables ending in a consonant, follow the ordinary rule, and add *no* termination for the plural, as et Ark, *ark*, or *sheet*, pl. Ark; et Flag, *a flag*, pl. Flag.

Some **add e**, as et Brev, a letter, pl. Breve.

Non-substantives used as substantives take **er** for the plural, as Ingen Menner, *no 'buts'*; Lutter Neier, *unqualified 'noes.'*

Remarks on the Plural of Substantives.

Proper names, abstract substantives, nouns of multitude and material, naturally have *no* plural. But, under certain circumstances, they can be used as plurals, e. g.

Proper names used to represent a class of attributes, which then take a plural in **er**.

> Dem Tordenskjold lærte at vove,
> af Jueler de lærte at Slaa.
> *For Tordenskjold taught them to dare all,*
> *From Juel they learnt how to smile.*
> literally, *Juels, men like Nils Juel.*

Abstract nouns to denote individuals; as

> Skjønheder, *beauties.*   Berømtheder, *celebrities.*

Some substantives that have a plural are used **collectively** in the **singular**; as

> han ligger her og skyder Rype (for Ryper) om Vinteren, *he stays here and shoots grouse in the winter.*
> al den Fugl han fik, *all the birds he shot.*
> en Mængde Lax, Ørret, *a mass of salmon, of trout.*

And with numerals:

> ti Mand, *ten men*; ti Fod, *ten foot*; fem Skilling, *five shillings*. So in English we speak of *a ten foot rule, a five shilling piece*.

But such nouns, if they **end in e**, are used always in the plural; as

> tre Kroner, *three crowns*.

But they say both

> syv Mil, and, syv Mile, *seven mile*, or *seven miles*.
> paa mange Mil, *for many a mile*.

Folk is used both as a singular and as a plural; e. g.

> Plur. mange Folk, *many people*; rige Folk, *rich people*.
> Sing. hvor godt Folk er, kommer godt Folk efter, *where good folk are come good folk after*.

ADJECTIVES.

The Adjective has two forms. 1. the strong form. 2. the weak form.

The strong form adds **t** for the neuter, and **e** for the plural.

The weak form always ends in **e**.

The strong form is used after the Indefinite Article.

The weak form is used after the Definite Article.

The Adjective agrees in gender and number with its substantive.

en god Mand, *a good man.*   gode Mænd.
et godt Barn, *a good child.*   gode Børn.
den gode Mand, *the good man.*   de gode Mænd.
det gode Barn, *the good child.*   de gode Børn.
Manden er god, *the man is good.*   Mændene ere gode.
Barnet er godt, *the child is good.*   Børnene ere gode.

STRONG FORM. (INDEFINITE.)

          Sing.   Plur.

Common { N. en ung Pige, *a young girl.*   unge Piger, *young girls.*
         { G. en ung Piges.   unge Pigers.

Neuter { N. et ungt Barn, *a young child.*   unge Børn.
       { G. et ungt Barns.   unge Børns.

WEAK FORM. (DEFINITE.)

          Sing.   Plur.

Common { N. den unge Pige, *the young girl.*   de unge Piger.
         { G. den unge Piges.   de unge Pigers.

Neuter { N. det unge Barn, *the young child.*   de unge Børn.
       { G. det unge Barns.   de unge Børns.

Participles ending in **en**, make **et** in the neut. sing. indef. and **ne** in the plural; as

ADJECTIVES.

INDEFINITE.

Sing.	Plur.
en voxen Quinde, *a grown-up woman.*	voxne Quinder.
et voxet Menneske, *an adult.*	voxne Mennesker.

DEFINITE.

den voxne Quinde.	de voxne Quinder.
det voxne Menneske.	de voxne Mennesker.

Obs. In Old Norse the Adj. had special terminations for the three genders, and for four cases.

The nomin. masc. ended in r, godr; the accus. masc. in an, godan; hence comes the termination en, in such expressions in poetry as

Herr Sinklar drog over salten Hav.
Naar Harpen tier ved breden Bord.
I vilden hoien Sky.

Hence it is plain that megen, *great*, nogen, *some*, liden, *little*, ingen, *none*, are properly accusative cases.

The dat. neut. ended in u, godn; which is now represented by e in such expressions as iblinde, *blindfold*; tilgode, *due*; medrette, *justly*.

(See above, p. 22, l. 15.)

The adj. liden, *little*, is irregular: it has for the neut. lidet, lidt (substantival); for the weak form, lille; and for the plural smaa; thus

en liden Gut, *a little boy.*

STRONG. (INDEFINITE.)

	Sing.	Plur.
Common	N. en liden, or lille Gut.	smaa Gutter.
	G. en liden, lille Guts.	smaa Gutters.
Neuter	N. et lidet, or lille Barn.	smaa Børn.
	G. et lidet, or lille Barns.	smaa Børns.

WEAK. (DEFINITE.)

	Sing.	Plur.
Common	N. den lille Gut.	de smaa Gutter.
	G. den lille Guts.	de smaa Gutters.
Neuter	N. det lille Barn.	de smaa Børn.
	G. det lille Barns.	de smaa Børns.

Obs. The neuter form 'lidt' has a positive meaning, and is equivalent to noget, *some*, as

> han er lidt ældre end sin Broder, *he is a little older than his brother;*

but

> han er lidet ældre end sin Broder, *he is only a little, not much, older than his brother.*

In old ballads the expression, den liden smaa Dreng, frequently occurs.

The weak form of the Adjective is used after den, *the*; min, *mine*; din, *thine*; sin, *his*; vor, *our*; jer, *your*; denne, *this*; hin, *yon*; hvilken, *which*; hver, *every*; as—

> min gode Ven, *my good friend.*
> hver evige Nat, *every mortal night.*

After a substantive in the genitive case; as

> Guds hellige Navn, *God's holy name.*
> Præstens smukke Datter, *the priest's pretty daughter.*

After the Def. Art. understood; as

> forrige Aar, *last year.*
> samme Mand, *the same man.*
> for ramme Alvor, *in sober earnest.*
> Halfdan Svarte, *Halfdan the black.*
> (In Old Norse, Halfdan hinn Svarte.)

Before the Def. Art.; as

> hele Dagen, *all the day.*
> et Skud af gamle Kjæmpe stammen, *a scion of the old warrior stock.*

In exclamations; as

> arme Mand, *poor man!*
> rige Knut, du lever godt, *rich Knut, you are well off!*

On the Inflection of Adjectives.

GENDER. Adjectives ending in **en** or **n** drop **n** before **t** in the neuter; as

> liden, lidet, *little*; egen, eget, *own*; megen, meget, *great*; nogen, noget, *some*; anden, andet, *other*; hvilken, hvilket, *which*; min, mit,; din, dit; sin, sit; den, det.

ADJECTIVES.

Also the Past Participles passive of verbs; as

skreven, skrevet, *written.*

Adjectives that end in a vowel, or in d preceded by a long vowel, shorten the vowel in the neuter, as

nȳ, nȳt, *new*; grāā, grāăt, *gray*; blāā, blăăt, *blue*; gōd, gŏdt, *good*; flād, flădt, *flat*; blød, blødt, *soft.*

When a strong Particip. has assumed the nature of an Adject. it retains n in the neut.; as

et drukkent Menneske, *a drunkard.*
et velkomment Brev, *a welcome letter.*

The following are not inflected in the neuter:—

1. Adj. ending in t, as en kort Vei, et kort Sværd.

Derivative Adjectives in sk, as et krigersk Folk, *a warlike people*: but stem-words in sk take t, as et falskt Menneske, *a double dealer*; færskt Tømmer, *unseasoned timber.*

2. Many adjectives ending in d, preceded by a Vowel; as

glad, *glad*; ræd, *afraid*; fremmed, *foreign*; as, et fremmed Land.

Some in which the d follows a consonant are used both with and without the final t; as

et lærd Værk, *a learned work.*
det er ikke Umagen værdt, *it is not worth the trouble.*

3. Adjectives that end in a Vowel; as

ædru, *sober*; øde, *waste*; ringe, *insignificant*; bange, *afraid*; stille, *quiet.*

Except those ending in aa; as raat Kjød, *raw meat.*
and fri, which makes frit, *free*, and ny, nyt, *new.*

In the Norwegian peasant language we have also

det blev stilt, *stillness ensued.*
det er saa ødt her, *it is so desolate here.*

NUMBER. Adjectives ending in a single consonant, preceded by a short root-vowel, double the final consonant in the plural, as let, *easy*, weak form lette ; from, *gentle*, fromme.

Adjectives ending in el, en, er, lose the e preceding l, n, r, when a final e is added ; as

> gammel, gamle, *old*; fager, fagre, *fair*; doven, dovne, *stupid*; skreven, skrevne, *written*.

Participles ending in et have the same form in the common gender and in the neuter; and ede for the plural, and weak form ; as

> en elsket Søn, *a beloved son*, et elsket Barn, elskede Sønner.

Participles ending in t preceded by a consonant add e for the plur. and weak form, as, fordømt, *condemned*; de fordømte, *the damned*.

The weak Past Part. originally ended in d in the common gender, elsked, *loved*. In the spoken language, and occasionally in writing, the Past Participles of many verbs are made to end in d for both genders.

The final e of the plural is slurred over in pronunciation in words ending in aa. Faa, *few*, and smaa, *small*, are used only in the plural; e. g.

> med faa Ord, *briefly*. de smaa Profeter, *the minor prophets*.

There is a neut. form, smaat, in use however ; as

> det er smaat for ham, *he is in straitened circumstances*.
> jeg har saa smaat Lyst til at spørge hende, *I have half a mind to ask her*.

Some adjectives are indeclinable.

1. Those that end in e ; as

> ringe, *small*; bange, *afraid*; nøie, *exact*.

2. in es or s preceded by a consonant ; as

> et afsides Sted, *a retired spot*.

et middels Aar, *an average year.*
nymodens Hatte, *fashionable hats.*
vor fælles Ven, *our mutual friend.*

3. the Adjectives lutter, mere, kvit; as

ikke kunne se Skoven for lutter Træer, *not to be able to see the wood for trees.*
vi bleve ham kvit, *we got rid of him.*

gjængs; as,

et gjængs Udtryk, *a current expression*;

but the weak form is also found; as,

Ordet er endnu gjængse paa Landet, *the word is still in use in the country.*

tilfreds, *contented*, as,

et tilfreds Sind, *a contented mind*;

but also

den tilfredse Mand.

gammeldags, *antique*; as,

sorte Heste med gammeldags Sadler, *black horses with old-fashioned saddles*;

but also

gammeldagse Dragter, *antique dresses.*

Comparison of Adjectives.

The COMPARATIVE is formed by adding ere to the root form, or common gender of the positive; as

et smukkere Barn, *a prettier child*;
lærdere Personer, *more learned persons.*

The comparative is not inflected in gender or number.

The SUPERLATIVE is formed by adding est; as

kort, kortere, kortest, *short, shorter, shortest.*

The superlative distinguishes the definite form by adding e, but is otherwise uninflected.

The degrees of comparison may also be expressed by **mere**, **mest**, *more* and *most*.

Adjectives which in the positive drop **e**, or double the final consonant, follow the same rule in forming the comparative and superlative; as

> ædel, ædlere, ædlest, *noble, nobler, noblest*. glat, *smooth*, glattere, glattest.

Derivatives in **ig, lig, som**, admit only **st** (not **est**) in the superlative; as

> ærlig, *honest*, ærligere, ærligst. virksom, *active*, virksommere, virksomst.

Those that end in **e**, add **re, st**; as

> ringe, ringere, ringest.

Some adjectives have the stem-vowel modified in forming the degrees of comparison; as

lang *neut.*	langt, *long*	længere	længst
stor ,,	stort, *big*	større	størst
ung ,,	ungt, *young*	yngre	yngst
faa ,,	*few*	færre	færrest
tung ,,	tungt, *heavy.*	tyngre tungere	tyngst, tungest

Fager, *fair*, makes feirest, as well as fagrest, in the superlative.

Nær *near*, makes nærmere, nærmest, næst.

These form the comparative and superlative from a different root.

gammel, *neut.*	gammelt, *old*	ældre	ældst
god, ,,	godt, *good*	bedre	bedst,
liden, ,,	lidet, *little*	mindre	mindst
mange ,,	*many*	flere	flest
megen ,,	meget, *much*	mere, mer	mest
ond ,,	ondt, *bad* ⎫		
slem ,,	slemt ⎬	værre	værst
ilde	⎪		
daarlig ,,	daarligt ⎭		

ADJECTIVES.

The following, derived from Adverbs, are used only in the comparative and superlative.

(Bag), *behind*	bagre	bagerst, *hindmost.*
(Bort-e), *away*	bortre	borterst, *furthermost.*
(ind-e), *in*	indre	inderst, *inmost.*
(midt), *middle*	midtre	midterst, *midmost.*
(ned-e), *down*	nedre	nederst, *lowermost.*
(ov-en), *over*	øvre	øverst, *uppermost.*
(ud-e), *out*	ydre	yderst, *outermost.*

Høire, *right*, and venstre, *left*, are properly comparatives.
The following occur only in the superlative—

(for, *before*)	forrest, *foremost.*
(før, *before*)	først, *first.*
(siden, *afterwards*)	sidst, *last.*
(oppe, *up*)	ypperst, *highest.*
(under, *beneath*)	underst, *undermost.*
(mellem, *between*)	mellemst, *midmost.*
(agter, *behind*)	agterst, *hindmost.*
(een, *one*)	eneste, *only.*

The following do not admit of inflection for the degrees of comparison:

Adjectives with derivative endings in **en, et, sk, es, s**, after a consonant; as

gnaven, *fretful*; ulden, *woollen*; bakket, *hilly*; skjægget, *bearded*; dyrisk, *brutish*; udvortes, *external*; stakkels, *poor*; eens, *single*; fremmed, *foreign.*

Participles, as levende, elsket; except those that have become Adjectives; as

berømt, *renowned*	berømtere	berømtest
bestemt, *definite*	bestemtere	bestemtest

In these cases the comparative and superlative are formed by the aid of mere and mest; e. g.

der gives ikke en mere vredladen og frygtelig Skabning til i hele Naturen, *there is not a more ferocious and terrible creature in the world.*

The comparative always has the weak form, ending in **e**; as

en større Del, *a larger part.*

The superlative takes the termination **e** when it stands before a Substantive, usually with the Def. Art. ; as

den mægtigste Mand, *the mightiest man.*
Aarets længste Dag, *the longest day in the year.*
for første og sidste Gang, *for the first and last time.*

When it stands as a predicate, it generally takes the strong, or uninflected form ; as

enhver er sig selv nærmest : *every one is nearest to himself.*
Dagene ere kortest om Vinteren, *the days are shortest in winter* ;

but, on account of the Def. Art. preceding,

han var den ældste, *he was the eldest.*

The strong form is also used in the following phrases:—

hvad har Du mest Lyst til ? *What do you fancy most?*
De kunde faa Lov til at tage sig til, det de vilde og havde bedst Lyst til, *they could get leave to take what they liked best.*

Sometimes the strong form implies a somewhat different meaning from the weak ; as

Jeg skal gjøre det med **største** Fornøielse, *I will do it with very great pleasure* ;
med størst Fornøielse, *with greater pleasure (than I should do something else.)*

The superlative is often intensified by **aller** prefixed; as

allerkjærest, *most dearly.* allersidst, *the very last.*

NUMERALS.

Cardinal.	Ordinal.	
1 een, *com.* eet, *neut.* den ene. det ene.	den, det første,	1ste.
2 to (tvende).	den anden, det andet	2den.
3 tre (trende).	den, det, tredie,	3die.
4 fire.	„ fjerde,	4de.
5 fem.	„ femte.	5te.
6 sex, seks.	„ sjette,	6te.
7 syv.	„ syvende,	7de.
8 aatte, otte.	„ ottende,	8de.
9 ni.	„ niende,	9de.
10 ti.	„ tiende,	10de.
11 elleve.	„ ellevte,	11te.
12 tolv.	„ tolvte,	12te.
13 tretten.	„ trettende,	13de.
14 fjorten,	„ fjortende,	14de.
15 femten.	„ femtende,	15de.
16 seksten, seisten.	„ sekstende,	16de.
17 sytten.	„ syttende,	17de.
18 atten.	„ attende,	18de.
19 nitten.	„ nittende,	19de.
20 tyve.	„ tyvende,	20de.
21 een og tyve.	„ en og tyvende,	21de.
30 tredive.	„ tredivte,	30te.
40 fyrreti, fyrretyve.	„ fyrretyvende,	40de.
50 femti. halvtreds. halvtredsindstyve.	„ femtiende, halvtresindstyvende	50de.
60 seksti. tres (colloquial). tresindstyve.	„ sekstiende, tresindstyvende	60de.
70 sytti. halvfjerds. halvfjerdsindstyve.	„ syttiende, halvfjerdsindstyvende	70de.
80 otti.	„ ottiende,	80de.

Cardinal.	Ordinal.

firs (coll.).
firsindstyve.   den, det, firsindstyvende
90 nitti.   „ nittiende,   90de.
halvfems.
halvfemsindstyve.   „ halvfemsindstyvende
100 hundrede.   „ hundrede,   100de.
101 hundrede og een.   ., hundrede og første,   101te.
200 to hundrede   ,, to hundrede,   200de.
1000 tusinde.   ,, tusinde.

een Gang, *once*.   første Gang, *1st time*.
to Gange, *twice*.   anden Gang, *2nd time*.
tre Gange, *thrice*.   tredie Gang, *3rd time*.

for det første, *firstly*.
for det andet, *secondly*.
for det tredie, *thirdly*.

¼ en Fjerdedeel.   en Fjerdedeels Mil, ¼ *of a mile*.
½ en halv.   en Halvmil, ½ *a mile*.
1½ halvanden.   halvanden Mil, 1½ *mile*.
2½ halvtredie.   halvtredie Mil, 2½ *miles*.
⅔ to trediedele.   to trediedeels Mil, ⅔ *of a mile*.
2⅓ to en trediedeel.   to en trediedeel Mil, 2⅓ *miles*.

½ is an adjective, en halv, et halvt, den halve, det halve. En halv time, *half an hour*. En og halv Mil, *one and a half mile*; halv veis, *half way*. En Fjerdings Vei, *a ¼ of a mile Norsk*, equal to 1¾ mile English.

et Par, *a pair*, et Par Støvler, *a pair of boots*. et Par Timer, *a couple of hours*.

et Dusin, et Tylft, *a dozen*.
et Snees, *a score*, as, to Snes Ørred, *two score trout*.
en Skok, *three score*, en hel Skok, *a whole heap*, or *crowd*.

REMARKS ON THE NUMERALS.

In the Northern and Western parts of Norway, as in Old Norse, in Swedish, and in English, the Numeration is made by *tens*.

NUMERALS.

But in Southern Norway and in Denmark, from 50 onward to 100, the Numeration is counted by *twenties*; hence we have:—

halvtredsindstyve, i. e. *three times twenty all but half twenty* = 50.
tresindstyve, *three times twenty* = 60.
halvfjerdsindstyve, *four times twenty all but half-twenty* = 70.
firsindstyve, *four times twenty* = 80.
halvfemsindstyve, *five times twenty all but half-twenty* = 90.

and in a shortened form

halvtreds, 50: tres, 60: halvfjerds, 70: firs, 80: halvfems, 90.

The ordinals, after *first* and *second*, are inflected in the weak form e; as

den tredie Dag, *the third day.*
det nittende Aarhundrede, *the nineteenth century.*
hvert fjerde Aar, *every fourth year.*
min tredivte Fødselsdag, *my thirteenth birthday.*

Examples.

et Brev under dato nittende Januar, *a letter dated the 19th of January.*
hvilken dato er det idag? *What day of the month is it to-day?*
den er den en og tyvende Juli, *it is the 21st of July.*
hvad er Klokken? *What o'clock is it?*
det mangler ti Minuter i halv tre, *it is twenty minutes past two.*
Klokken er tolv, *it is twelve o'clock.*
den er tre kvarteer til eet, *it is a quarter to one.*
fem Minuter over seks, *five minutes past six.*
Dampen reiser ti Minuter over fire, *the steamer starts at ten minutes past four.*
fem Minuter paa syv, *five minutes to seven.*

PRONOUNS.

PERSONAL.

First Person.

	Sing.	Plur.
N.	Jeg, *I.*	vi, *we.*
G.		vores, *ours.*
D. A.	mig, *me.*	os, *us.*

Second Person.

	Sing.	Plur.	
N.	Du, *thou.*	I, *ye.*	De, *you.*
G.		eders, Jeres,	Deres, *yours.*
D. A.	Dig, *thee.*	eder, Jer, *ye.*	Dem, *you.*

Third Person.

	Sing.	Plur.
N.	Han, *he*; hun, *she.*	de, *they.*
G.	Hans, *his*; hendes, *hers.*	deres, *theirs.*
D. A.	Ham, *him*; hende, *her.*	dem, *them.*
N.	den, det, *it.*	de, *they.*
G.	dens, dets, *its.*	deres, *theirs.*
D. A.	den, det, *it.*	dem, *them.*

I, *ye,* is used chiefly in biblical language.

Du, *thou,* is used among familiar friends, and in speaking to children and servants.

De, Deres, Dem, *you,* spelt with a capital letter, is used in ordinary conversation, and takes the verb in the singular; as

    De der! *you there!*
    hvad siger De? *what say you?*
    nu see, Far, kom og sæt Dem her, *See now, father, come and sit you down here,* Dem being used instead of dig.

In the spoken language Dere, pl. nom. and acc., *you,* is used in addressing several persons.

Han, *he*; hun, *she*, are used in Norse in coaxing, or familiar style for the second person; as

see her, Moder, der har hun to Duer som hun kan stege til Farbroder imorgen, *Look here, mother, here are two pigeons which you can roast for uncle to-morrow.*

REFLEXIVE.

The reflexive Pronoun of the third person is sig, *himself, herself, itself, themselves*; as

hun stødte sig, *she hurt herself.*

The genitive is represented by the Possessive Pronoun sin, sit; as

Manden slog sin Kone, *the man struck his wife.*

The first and second persons take the oblique cases of the corresponding Personal Pronouns.

De, *you*, takes the Verb in the singular, and is followed by Dem, not by sig; as

De har skadet Dem, *you have hurt yourself.*

1st Person.	jeg roser mig,	*I praise myself.*
	vi rose os,	*we praise ourselves.*
2nd Person.	du roser dig,	*thou praisest thyself.*
	De roser Dem,	*you praise yourself.*
	I rose Eder,	*you praise yourselves.*
3rd Person.	han roser sig,	*he praises himself.*
	hun roser sig,	*she praises herself.*
	den, det, roser sig,	*it praises itself.*
	de rose sig,	*they praise themselves.*
Infinitive.	At rose sig,	*to praise oneself.*

Selv may be added to all three persons, in both numbers, and all cases except the genitive; as

om jeg selv skal sige det, *though I say it that should not.*
du bør gjøre det selv, *you ought to do it yourself.*
han har selv Børn, *he has children of his own.*
vi bager selv vores Brød, *we bake our own bread.*
de talte bare om sig selv, *they talked only about themselves.*
bestem selv en Dag, *name your own day.*

The weak form is used before a Substantive with the Def. Art. suffixed; as

Selve Kongen, *the king himself.*

RECIPROCAL.

N.D.A. hinanden, *each other*; hverandre, *one another.*
G. hinandens, *each other's*; hverandres, *one another's*; as

vi, I, de elske hinanden, *love each other.*
Pigerne saae urolig paa hverandre, *the girls looked uneasily at one another.*

POSSESSIVE.

	Common.	Neuter.		
Sing.	min,	mit,	Plur.	mine, *my, mine.*
	din,	dit,		dine, *thy, thine.*
	Deres,			*yours.*
	sin,	sit,		sine, *his, hers, its, theirs.*
	vor,	vort,		vore, vores, *our, ours.*
	Jer,	Jert,		Jere, Eders, *your, yours.*
	egen,	eget,		egne, *own.*

In the first person the Possessive Pronoun vor, *our*, is more common than the genitive vores.

In the second person, conversely, Eders is commonly used, Jer seldom.

Possessive Pronouns, like other Adjs., when used substantively, take a genitive case, as

Mit og Mines Ve og Vel, *the weal and woe of me and mine.*

Note. The Personal Pronoun is used instead of the Possessive, when the substantive comes before the preposition, as

en Slætning af os, *a relation of ours.*

In the every-day language of the people the Possessive Pronoun is frequently placed after its substantive, the Def. Art. being suffixed; as

naar Gutten vaagnede tog han Duggen sin, *when the boy awoke he took his cloth.*
der seer du Gaarden min, *there you see my house.*

The genitive of the Personal Pronouns is similarly used; as

der var ingen som vilde kjøbe Hesten hans, *there was no one who would buy his horse.*

Examples.

det er ikke min Forretning, *it is not my business.*
I vort Land, *in our country.*
hvor er Deres Kuffert? *where is your trunk?*
Huset er mit, *the house is mine.*
en af vore Kammerater, *one of our comrades.*

DEMONSTRATIVE.

This.

		Common.	Neuter.		
Sing.	N.	denne,	dette, *this.*	Plur.	disse, *these.*
	G.	dennes,	dettes.		disses.
	D.A.	denne,	dette.		disse.

That.

Sing.	N.	den,	det, *that.*	de, *those.*
	G.	dens,	dets.	deres.
	D.A.	den,	det.	dem.

Yonder.

Sing.	N.	hin,	hint, *yon.*	hine, *those yonder.*
	G.	(hins),	(hints).	hines.
	D.A.	hin,	hint.	hine.

When these Pronouns are used adjectivally, they are inflected as Adjectives; as

disse Mænds Fortjenester, *these men's services.*
de Dages Mennesker, *the men of those days.*

Den and denne may be strengthened by the addition of der and her; as

den der, *that one there.* disse her, *these here.*

Hin is mostly confined to the written language; den, det, de, or den, der, being used in speaking; as

i de Dage, *in those days.*

Den, det, de, originally demonstrative, is used in four ways.

1. As Demonstrative, with accent, *that, those.*
2. As Personal Pronoun, *he, it, they.*
3. To express the second person sing., *you,* instead of the familiar du, *thou.* De, Deres, Dem, is used in ordinary conversation.
4. As Def. Art. before Adjectives, *the.*

Examples.

denne Hest er min, *this horse is mine.*
dette er min Hest, *this is my horse.*
disse Heste ere mine, *these horses are mine.*
dette Liv, hint Liv, *this life, the life to come.*
det har jeg længe vidst, *that I have known for a long time.*
den som du søger er ikke her, *he whom you seek is not here.*
den Vei skal vi alle, *that way we shall all go.*
vil De ikke sidde paa denne Stol? *won't you sit upon this chair?*
nei, jeg vil heller have den, *no, I would rather have that one.*
men denne her er bedre, *but this one is better.*
jeg troer det, *I believe so.*
jeg haaber det, *I hope so.*
disse meget fromme Folk, *your very pious people.*

In the written language the Substantive defined by a Demonstrative Pronoun, takes no Art., as den Tid, *that time*; denne Baad, *this boat*: but in talking they suffix the Def. Art. to the Substantive as well; as

den Veien er ikke saa bakket, *that road is not so hilly.*
det var det Svar jeg fik af de Karlene, *that was the answer I got from those fellows.*

Other demonstrative words are,

Saa, properly an Adverb, used adjectivally as a demonstrative in such expressions; as

i saa Tilfælde, *in that case.* in saa Maade, *in that way.*

Saadan, neut. saadant: pl. saadanne, *such.*

en saadan Mand, *or,* saadan en Mand, *such a man.*
et saadant Svar, *such an answer.*
Himmeriges Rige hører saadanne til, *of such is the kingdom of heaven.*

Adverbially:—
saadan gaaer det i Verden, *such is the way of the world.*

Slig, neut. sligt, pl. slige, *such.*
en slig Mand, *such a man.*   slige Folk, *such people.*

Samme:—
den samme Mand, *the same man.*
paa samme Maade, *in the same manner.*
det er mig det samme, *it's all the same to me.*
nu kan det være det samme med Brevet, *never mind the letter now.*
i selv samme Stund, *in the self same hour.*

Begge, *both,* genit. begges.
vi begge, *both of us.*
begge to, *both.*
med begge Hænder, *with both hands.*
begge Brødrene, *both the brothers.*
en for begge og begge for en, *jointly and separately.*

Obs. An archaic form is baade, med baade Hænder, also used as a conjunction; as han er større end baade du og jeg, *he is taller than either you or I.*

INTERROGATIVE.

The Interrogative Pronouns are hvo, *who?* hvem, *who?* hvilken, *which?* hvad, *what?*

Substantive:

Common.	Neuter.
N. hvo, hvem, *who?*	hvad, *what?*
G. hvis, *whose?*	
A. hvem, *whom?*	hvad, *what?*

Hvem, as nominative, is more common than hvo, in the spoken language; as

hvem er der, *who's there.*

E

Adjective.

> Sing. N. hvilken, hvilket, *which?*   Plur. hvilke, *which?*

The following are common forms expressing curiosity, wonder, contempt, &c.

> hvilken en Nar! *what a fool!*
> hvilken Daarskab! *what folly!*
> hvad for en Karl er du, *or,* hvad er du for en Karl, *what kind of fellow are you?*
> hvad var det for en Støi, *what noise was that?*
> hvad for noget er det, *what is that?*
> hvad der sidder for et Handelshoved paa den Dreng! *what a head for business the lad has!*
> han vidste ikke hvad Ben han skulde staa paa, *he knew not which leg to stand upon.*
> hvad Nyt, *what news?*
> hvad Andet, *what else?*
> hvem Anden skulde jeg møde end Peder selv, *whom else should I meet than Peter himself.*
> mon han lever endnu, *I wonder if he is still alive.*
> hvor mon han boer? *where does he live I wonder?*
> mon hvem der har gjort det, *I wonder who has done it.*
> mon hvad der kan være i Veien? *what can there be in the way, I wonder?*
> mon hvad dette betyder? *what can be the meaning of this, I wonder?*

RELATIVES.

The Relative Pronouns are

> N. Som, der, hvilken, *who, that, which.*
> G. hvis, *whose.*
> A. som, hvem, hvilken, *whom, that, which.*

Hvilken makes neut. **hvilket**, pl. **hvilke**.

Der is used for all genders and numbers, but only as a nominative case; as

> det skal være et klogt Barn der kjender sin egen Fader, *it must be a clever child that knows his own father.*

PRONOUNS.

Hvis is the genitive for both numbers and all genders; as

en Mand paa hvis Ord man kan stole, *a man whose word one can rely upon.*

Hvem, *whom*, is used for both singular and plural, but only of persons in the accusative case; as

en Mand paa hvem man can stole, *a man upon whom one can rely.*

Som is used for all numbers, genders, and cases, except the genitive; as

det som du saae, *that which you saw.*
de som ere tilstede, *they that are present.*

Som is the most commonly used of all the relatives. **Som** cannot take a Preposition before it, thus we must say,

de Ting, eller Mennesker som vi talte om, or hvorom vi talte, not, om som, *the things and persons we were talking about.*
han mødte den Mand som han havde spurgt efter, not, efter som, *the man whom he had asked after.*

Obs. The Antecedent is not expressed by a Personal Pronoun as in English, but by a Demonstrative, *he who deceives*, is den, not, han, som sviger. Nor by the Definite Article, except in certain cases, *light is the burden that another bears,* is, let er den Byrde, not Byrden, som en Anden bærer. The antecedent is marked by the Def. Art. suffixed, when an additional fact is predicated concerning it, and no classification or generalization is intended, e. g.

Manden som havde det lille Dukketheater blev fornøiet, *the man who owned the marionettes was overjoyed.*

Manden der havde gjort Komedie gik hen til sit lille Theater, *the man who had worked the show went to look after his little theatre.* Here, **den Mand som** would emphasize the distinction between that man and other men more than is required by the context.

Der, *who*, is used for the sake of variety, and to avoid the too frequent recurrence of **som**, e. g.

alle hilste paa ham som paa en der meget længe har været borte, *all greeted him as one who had been absent a long time.*

Hvem, *whom,* in the accusative case, can be used for the same purpose, as

> selv Forpagteren, hvem jeg agter som en Mand der besidder dyb Indsigt i mange Ting, har ikke kunnet løse denne Opgave, *the tenant, whom I respect as a man possessing deep insight in many matters, has not been able to solve this problem.*

Hvilken refers to persons and things. It may have the sentence as antecedent to it in the neuter; as

> hun kan vente hvilket jeg ikke kan, *she can wait, which I cannot.*

Or, it may be used with a substantive in apposition to the sentence; as

> Fjenden havde forsømt at udstille Vagter, en Uforsigtighed som, or, hvilken Uforsigtighed, senere viste sig skjæbnesvanger, *the enemy had omitted to post sentinels, an imprudence which, or, which imprudence, later on proved fatal.*

The Relative, as in English, is frequently omitted, chiefly in the following cases;

1. Where it would not be subject in a co-ordinate sentence; as

> hvad er det jeg hører? *what is that I hear?*
> hvem var det du talte med? *who was that you were talking to?*

2. Where it follows a superlative:

> den eneste Ko han eiede blev funden død, *the only cow he owned was found dead.*

3. When the Demonstrative Adverb **her,** or **der,** comes first in a co-ordinate sentence, the Relative in the nominative case may be omitted; as

> den Mand der gaar, *the man there is a-walking yonder.*

Analogous expressions in English are ' *the uproar there was,*' ' *the noise there is,*' ' *the fish there are in the river.*'

Examples of various uses of the Relative.

> jeg kjender ingen, som jeg med Sikkerhed kan betro dette Hverv, *I know no one that I can safely trust with this charge.*

det Eneste som han er bange for er Mester Erik, *the only thing he is afraid of is Mr. Erik.*

jeg træffer saa sjelden et Menneske med hvem jeg kan faa en ret fornuftig Samtale, *I so seldom meet a soul with whom I can have a good sensible talk.*

den ler bedst som ler sidst, *he laughs best who laughs last.*

den veed bedst hvor Skoen trykker, som har den paa, *he knows best where the shoe pinches who has it on.*

han er ikke længer den Mand han engang var, *he is no longer the man he once was.*

det er noget du ikke forstaar dig paa, lille Mand, *it is something you don't understand about, my little man.*

nu skal du høre alle de Steder jeg har været idag, *now you shall hear all the places I have been at to-day.*

den Sten man ei kan løfte skal man lade ligge, *the stone one cannot lift, one must let lie.*

denne Sten som ingen har kunnet løfte, *that stone which no one has been able to lift.*

han var den vittigste Mand jeg har kjendt, *he was the cleverest man I ever knew.*

lad dine Øine falde paa den Kurv der staar, *cast your eyes upon that basket standing there.*

lad ei Ven vide det Uven ei maa vide, *let not friend know what foe may not know.*

hvem er det du søger, *who is it you are looking for?*

det jeg skrev, skrev jeg, *what I have written I have written.*

Børnene, dem han elskede saa høit, *the children, those he loved so dearly.*

Indefinite Relatives.

The addition of **som**, or **der**, like the English *ever, soever,* gives an indefinite signification to the Relatives **hvo, hvem, hvad, hvilken, hvo som, hvem som, hvo der, hvem der, hvilken der,** *whoever, any one who, every one who,* **hvad som, hvad der, hvilket der,** *whatever, anything, everything which.*

hvo som angriber min Ære, over ham kræver jeg Hevn, *whoso attacks my honour, upon him I demand vengeance.*

hvad der er Ret skal være Ret, *whatever is right is right.*

jeg tager imod hvilke Tilbud der gjøres mig, *I will accept any offer that is made to me.*

Som, der, are omitted,

1. When the indefinite Relative is in the objective case; as

du kan uræd tale med Kongen hvad du lyster, *you can say to the king whatever you like, without fear.*

2. Also when the Pronoun stands as a subject of sentence, in which case the Verb must come last; as

hvo lidet saar han lidet faar, *whoso soweth little shall reap little.*

Examples of Indefinite Relative.

hvo som vover han vinder, *whoso ventures wins.*

jeg har gjort hvad der kunde gjøres, *I have done whatever could be done.*

jeg har gjort hvad jeg kunde, *I have done whatever I could.*

han kan maale sig med hvem det skal være, *he is a match for any one soever.*

du kan tage hvilken Vei du vil, *you can take whichever way you like.*

hvad med Synden kommer, med Sorgen bortgaar, *what comes with sin goes out with sorrow.*

Alt hvad jeg har, *or,* alt det som jeg har, *or,* alt det jeg har, *or,* alt jeg har, *all that I have.*

han kan læse hvilken Bog det skal være, *or,* enhver Bog som det skal være, *he can read any book you like.*

hvo Kjernen vil spise maa Nødden først bide, *whoso wishes to eat the kernel must first crack the nut.*

INDEFINITE PRONOUNS.

1. Used as substantives only: det, *it;* man, *one, they;* en, *one.*

2. Used sometimes as substantives, sometimes as adjectives. Nogen, *some, any*; somme, *some*; ingen, *none*; mangen, *many a one*; anden, *other*; al, *all*; enhver, *every one*; enhversomhelst. *every one whatsoever*; hvilkensomhelst, *any one whatsoever*.

Det is used only as a nominative case; as

det er koldt, *it is cold*; det siges, *it is said*.

man is used only as a nominative;

man siger, *they say*.

The genitive is supplied by sin (reflexive), *one's*; the oblique cases by sig, *oneself*; e. g.

man maa henvende sig til Eieren, *you must apply to the owner.*

En (genitive ens), *one's*, is used among the Norsk common people instead of man; as

det kan En nok vide, *that one can well understand.*
naar det er hændt i Ens egen Slægt faar en tro det, *when it has happened in one's own family, one has to believe it.*

Sing. Nogen, *some, anybody*; noget, *some, anything.*
Plur. Nogle, *some*; nogen, *any.*
Genit. Nogens, nogles.

Nogensomhelst, nogetsomhelst, *any whatever.*

The plural of **nogen**, in the sense of *any*, is **nogen**, not **nogle**; as

har du nogen Penne? *have you any pens?*
jeg vidste ikke at han havde nogen Søskende, *I did not know that he had any brothers and sisters.*

In common conversation **nogen** is often used for **nogle**, in the sense of *some*.

In negative expressions, **ikke nogle** comes to mean *not many*: **ikke nogen**, *not any*; e. g.

Valgene have ikke endnu gaaet for sig i nogle af de vestlige og nordlige Amter, *the elections have not come off yet in many of the western and northern districts;*

but

> man har endnu ikke foretaget Valg i nogen af de vestlige Amter, *the voting has not yet taken place in any of the western districts.*

N. A. D. Somme, *some, several.*
G. Sommes.

> somme dansede til de laae som døde; nogle dansede til de faldt i Svime, *some danced till they lay as if dead, some danced till they fell from giddiness.*
> efter sommes Mening, *in the opinion of some.*

N. A. D. Ingen, *nobody*; intet, *nothing.* Pl. ingen.
G. Ingens.

> Penge havde han ingen af, *money he had none.*
> hvo intet vover intet vinder, *nothing venture nothing have.*
> ingenting, *nothing.*
> ingen-, intetsomhelst, *nothing at all.*

N. A. D. Mangen, *many a one*; mangt. Pl. mange.
G. Mangens.

> mangen ler med Munden og græder i Hjertet, *many a one laughs with the mouth and grieves in the heart.*
> mangen en Dag, *many a day.*
> mangt et Suk, *many a sigh.*

N. A. D. Anden, *other*; andet. Pl. andre.
G. Andens, andres.

> en Anden, *another.*
> den anden, *the other.*
> hvem anden, *who else?*
> hver anden dag, *every other day.*
> intet andet end Fordærvelse, *nothing else than ruin.*
> med andre Ord, *in other words.*
> et er at gjøre Forslaget, et andet at udføre det, *it is one thing to make a resolution, another thing to keep it.*

Obs. In common talk in Norway, they say den andre Dagen, *the next day,* instead of **den anden Dag,** and **det andre,** for **det andet.**

PRONOUNS.

N. D. A. Al; alt.   Pl. alle, *all.*
G. Alles.

    af al Magt, *with might and main.*
    al Verden, *all the world.*
    naar Alt kommer til Alt, *when all's said and done.*
    for alting ikke, *on no account whatever.*
    allerstørst, *biggest of all* (Old Norsk genitive plur. allra).

N. D. A. **hver**; neut. **hvert**; and **enhver, ethvert**, *each.*

G. **hvers, enhvers.**

    hvermand, *every man.*
    alle og enhver, *each and all.*
    hver eneste en, *every single one.*

In poetry **hver den** occurs for **enhver som**; as

        Men hver den Sten, de mure ved Dag,
        Den var om Natten borte.

        And every stone built up by day
        At night that stone was borne away.

Hver-, hvem-, neut. **hvadsomhelst,** *any soever.*
Hvilken-, neut. **hvilket-,** pl. **hvilkesomhelst;** as

    jeg tør binde an med hversomhelst, *I dare enter the lists with any one you like.*
    han tager tiltakke med hvadsomhelst, *he is contented, or, will put up with anything.*

VERBS.

The Verb, as in English, is conjugated partly by inflexion, partly by means of auxiliaries.

Inflexion is used to distinguish Number; as jeg elsker, *I love*; vi elske, *we love.*

Tense; as jeg elskede, *I loved*; elsket, *loved*; elskende, *loving.*

Mood; as Elsk, *love*; Gud hjælpe mig, *God help me.*

Voice; as jeg, vi, elskes, *I, we, are loved*; elskedes, *were loved*; at elskes, *to be loved.*

Auxiliary Verbs are used to express the tenses, other than the present and imperfect, of the active, and all the tenses of the passive voice; as

Active.

Perf. jeg har spurgt, *I have asked.*
Plup. jeg havde spurgt, *I had asked.*
Fut. jeg skal spørge, *I will ask.*
    han vil spørge, *he will ask.*
Fut. Perf. jeg skal have spurgt, *I shall have asked.*
    han vil have spurgt, *he will have asked.*
Conj. Imperf. jeg skulde spørge, *I should ask.*
    han vilde spørge, *he would ask.*
Plup. jeg skulde have spurgt, *I should have asked.*
    han vilde have spurgt, *he would have asked.*

Passive.

Pres. jeg elskes, *or*, bliver elsket, *I am loved.*
Past. jeg elskedes, *or*, blev elsket, *I was loved.*
    han spurgtes, *or*, blev spurgt, *he was asked.*
Perf. jeg er bleven elsket, *I have been loved.*

Plup. jeg var bleven elsket, *I had been loved.*
Fut. jeg skal spørges, *I shall be asked.*

Verbs of motion are conjugated by the help of at være. *to be*, instead of at have, in the compound tenses; as

jeg er kommen, *I am come.*
jeg var kommen, *I was come,* for, *I had come.*
at være kommen, *to be come, to have come.*

Number. The distinctive termination of the plural in e has gone out of use in the spoken language, and to a great extent in the written language also. Formerly the plural of the present and imperfect ended in e; as

jeg taler, *I talk*; vi tale, *we talk*; jeg var, *I was*; vi vare, *we were*;

they now say,

vi taler, *we talk*; vi var, *we were.*

In exalted style—in the Bible, for instance—the plural of the imperative ends in er; as giver, *give ye.* Elsewhere it is giv, the same as in the singular.

The dropping of these and other old forms is now advocated and adopted by literary critics of the advanced school.

Tense. The fundamental likeness of structure between the English and Norwegian languages is shown by the fact that in both it is only the present and imperfect that are denoted by inflexion.

jeg hører, *I hear*; jeg hørte, *I heard.*

Moods. The second person singular imperative is expressed by the stem form of the verb; as

læs høit, *read aloud*; hør du, *listen.*

The optative is identical in form with the infinitive; as

Man sige hvad man vil, *people may say what they like.*
Held følge ham, *good luck attend him.*

Obs. This mood is not much used in the literature of to-day. It is common in Old Norsk, and is still found in the language of the common people.

A wish is generally expressed by **gid**; as

gid han var her, *would that he were here.*

The infinitive is usually preceded by **at**, *to*, as, at sove, *to sleep*; at bindes, *to be tied*; and by, **for at**, to express a purpose, as, for at afvende Mistanken, *to ward off suspicion.*

At is omitted after maa, *must*; kan, *can*; bør, *ought*; lad, *let*; gid, *would that*; and faar in the sense of *must*, as, du faar se dig før, *you must* (lit. *have got to*) *look before you.*

The infinitive admits distinction of tenses, as, at læse, *to read*; at have læst, *to have read*; at ville, kunne, skulle læse, *to be about*, or, *able to read.*

In speaking, **at**, the sign of the infinitive is pronounced **aa**, the t being slurred over; but **at**, *that*, is always pronounced as written.

When the stem of the verb ends in **aa**, **e**, **o**, **y**, or **ø**, the terminal **e** is omitted, and the infinitive sounds exactly like the stem, as, **at gaa**, *to go*, not gaae; **at faa**, *to get*, not faae; **at le**, *to laugh*, not lee; **at tro**, *to believe*, not troe; **at sy**, *to sew*, not sye; **at dø**, *to die*, not døe; **at fri**, **at befri**, *to deliver*, not frie. But often verbs whose stem ends in i take **e**, as, **at bie**, *to abide*; **at tie**, *to be silent.*

Participle. The present active is formed by adding **ende** to the stem; as

den fiyvende Hollænder, *the flying dutchman*, from flyve, *to fly.*
Flere store Hunde sprang gjøende op, *several big dogs jumped up barking.*

This participle is not, as in English, used to form a tense; e. g.

hun spandt, *she was spinning.*
han stod og røgte, *he was standing smoking his pipe.*

The past participle passive of many strong Verbs, when joined to a Substantive, or when used as a predicate, is declined like an Adjective; as

en skreven Tale, *a written speech.*
et skrevet Brev, *a written letter.*
den skrevne Tale, *the written speech.*
de stjaalne Breve, *the stolen letters.*
Posten er kommen, *the post is come.*
et Brev er kommet til ham, *a letter is come for him.*

In speaking, this distinction of gender is commonly neglected and the form in t is used; as

Talen er skrevet, men endnu ikke holdt, *the speech has been written, but not delivered yet.*

But in the plural the concord is mostly observed; as

Talerne vare skrevne, *the speeches were written.*
De vare nær blevne tagne til Fange, *they were nearly taken prisoners.*

The past participle of the regular, or weak Verbs, ending in et, when used as an Adjective, changes et into ede in the plural and definite forms; as

jeg har elsket, *I have loved*; but, de elskede Børn, *the beloved children.*

Voice. The inflected passive in es has the force of an aorist tense; as

hvor Aadslet er, samles Ørnene, *where the carcass is there the eagles are gathered together.*
hendes Øine fyldtes med Taarer, *her eyes filled with tears.*

The following paradigm will show the formation of the various parts of the Verb; but it must be noted that in the spoken language the plural inflexion in e is neglected, and the form is the same for all persons singular and plural.

Also, that Verbs of motion are conjugated with the help of **vare** instead of **have**.

Also, that in the compound tenses the neuter of the participle is used without regard to the gender or number of the subject.

Active.

At bringe, *to bring*; bragte, bragt, *brought*.

INDICATIVE MOOD.

Present Tense.—*I bring, am bringing.*

  jeg bringer. vi bringe.
  du bringer. I bringe.
  han bringer. de bringe.

Imperfect.—*I brought, was bringing, did bring.*

  jeg vi ⎫
  du I ⎬ bragte.
  han de ⎭

Perfect.—*I have brought.*

jeg ⎫   vi ⎫
du ⎬ har bragt. I ⎬ have (har) bragt.
han ⎭   de ⎭

Pluperfect.—*I had brought.*

  jeg vi ⎫
  du I ⎬ havde bragt.
  han de ⎭

Future.—*I shall or will bring.*

jeg vil, *or* skal ⎫   vi ville, *or* skulle ⎫
du vil, skal ⎬ bringe. I ville, skulle ⎬ bringe.
han vil, skal ⎭   de ville, skulle ⎭

Future Perfect.—*I shall or will have brought,*

jeg vil, skal ⎫   vi ville, skulle ⎫
du vil, skal ⎬ have bragt. I ville, skulle ⎬ have bragt.
han vil, skal ⎭   de ville, skulle ⎭

also

  jeg ⎫   vi ⎫
  du ⎬ faar bragt.   I ⎬ faae bragt.
  han ⎭   de ⎭

VERBS. 63

Obs. This latter form is mostly used after conjunctions, such as **naar, da, dersom,** e. g.

naar jeg faar spist Aftenmad, *when I shall have eaten my supper.*

SUBJUNCTIVE OR CONDITIONAL.

Imperfect.—*Would or should bring.*

jeg vi
du I } vilde, *or,* skulde bringe.
han de

Pluperfect.—*Would or should have brought.*

jeg vi
du I } vilde, *or,* skulde have bragt.
han de

Also with auxil. faar, *when I had, or, should have brought.*

jeg vi
du I } fik bragt.
han de

This Pluperfect is mostly used after conjunctions, and in oratio obliqua; e. g. han sagde at naar han fik læst Bogen vilde han reise, *he said he would start as soon as he had finished the book.*

IMPERATIVE.

Bring (thou), bring (du).   *Bring (ye),* bringer (I).

OPTATIVE.

Let him bring, bringe.

INFINITIVE.

Present.—*To bring,* at bringe.

Perfect.—*To have brought,* at have bragt.

Future.—*To be going to bring,* at ville, *or,* skulle, *or,* være i Begreb at bringe.

PARTICIPLE.

Present.—*Bringing,* bringende.

Passive.

At binde, *to bind,* bandt; *neut.* bundet, *com.* -en, *plur.* -ne.

INDICATIVE.

Present.—*I am bound.*

jeg   vi
du   I   } bindes.
han   de

Also

jeg }   { bundet.   vi }   { bundet.
du   } bliver {   I } blive {
han }   { bunden.   de }   { bundne.
det   bundet.

Imperfect.—*I was bound.*

jeg   vi
du   I   } bandtes.
han   de

Also

jeg }   { bundet.   vi }   { bundet.
du   } blev {   I } blev {
han }   { bunden.   de }   { bundne.
det   bundet.

Perfect.—*I, you, he, &c. have been bound.*

Sing. jeg er bleven bundet *or* bunden.
     du er bleven bundet *or* bunden.
     han er bleven bundet *or* bunden.
     det er blevet bundet.

Plur. vi er *or* ere blevne bundet *or* bundne.
     I er *or* ere blevne bundet *or* bundne.
     de er *or* ere blevne bundet *or* bundne.

Also, the following combinations are used.

Sing. jeg, du, han, er blevet bundet *or* bunden.
     vi, I, de, er *or* ere blevet bundet *or* bundne.

Pluperfect.—*I, you, he, &c. had been bound.*

jeg, &c., var bleven bundet *or* bunden, *or* blevet bundet *or* bunden.
vi, &c., var *or* vare, blevne bundet *or* bundne, *or* blevet bundet *or* bundne.

VERBS.

Future.—*I shall be bound.*
jeg, du, han skal *or* vil bindes.
vi, I, de skulle *or* ville bindes.

jeg, &c., skal *or* vil blive bundet *or* bunden.
det skal *or* vil blive bundet.
vi, I, de skulle *or* ville blive bundet *or* bundne.

Future Perfect.—*I, &c., shall have been bound.*
jeg, &c., skal være blevet bundet *or* bunden.
det skal være blevet bundet.
vi, I, de skal *or* skulle være blevet bundet, *or* blevne bundet *or* bundne.

CONDITIONAL.

Imperfect.—*I should be bound.*
jeg, du, han, vi, I, de skulde bindes.

jeg, du, han skulde *or* vilde blive bundet *or* bunden.
det skulde *or* vilde blive bundet.
vi, I, de skulde *or* vilde blive bundet *or* bundne.

Pluperfect.—*I should have been bound.*
jeg, &c., skulde være blevet *or* bleven bundet *or* bunden.
det skulde være blevet bundet.
vi, I, de skulde være blevet *or* blevne bundet *or* bundne.

IMPERATIVE.

Be thou, or *ye, bound.*
Vær *or* bliv bundet.   Vær *or* værer I bundne.

OPTATIVE.

Would that I, thou, &c., were bound.
gid jeg, du, han var bundet.
gid vi, I, de være bundet *or* bundne.

INFINITIVE.

Present.—*To be bound,* at bindes, at blive bundet.
Perfect.—*To have been bound,* at være blevet bundet.
Future.—*To be going,* or, *about to be bound,* at skulle bindes.

Interrogative Form. In asking a question the Verb is placed before its subject; as

> sover han? *is he asleep?*
> sov han? *was he asleep?*
> har han sovet? *has he slept?*

Negative. In denials and in negative questions the Negative Particle is placed after the Verb; as

> han sover ikke, *he is not asleep.*
> han sov ikke, *he was not asleep.*
> han har ikke sovet, *he has not slept.*
> sover du ikke? *are you not asleep?*
> sov du ikke? *were you not asleep?*
> har du ikke sovet? *haven't you slept?*

Examples of the various parts of the Verb.

> Faderen havde jo lidt Penge, ikke sandt? *the father had some money, hadn't he?*
> hun havde havt to Sønner, sagde hun, men hun havde bare en igjen, *she had had two sons, she said, but she had only one left.*
> hvem har sagt han bor her? *who said he lives here?*
> Hunden er blevet dræbt, *the dog has been killed.*
> hvem har dræbt den? *who killed him?*
> har du nogensinde været i Bergen, *were you ever in Bergen?*
> ja, jeg har været der et Par Dage, *yes I was there a couple of days.*
> han følges bestandig af sin Hund, *he is always followed by his dog.*
> har De seet hans Hunde? de beundres af alle, *have you seen his dogs? they are admired by all.*
> Gutten var blevet puffet ud i Vandet, *the boy had been pushed into the water.*
> han blev trukket iland af Hunden, *he was pulled ashore by the dog.*
> to Børn er blevet frelste af den Hund. For en prægtig Hund! *two children have been saved by that dog. What a fine dog!*
> den blev dræbt af en Tyv, *he was killed by a thief.*
> jeg fandt den død; den var blevet dræbt med Gift, *I found him dead; he had been killed by poison.*

Tyven er blevet greben, *the thief has been caught.*

han burde straffes; han vil blive straffet, *he ought to be punished, he will be punished.*

Tyven kunde kanske være blevet sparet, hvis han havde sparet min Hund, *the thief might perhaps have been spared if he had spared my dog.*

en Dame og en Herre er komne, *a lady and a gentleman have arrived.*

en Dame og hendes Barn blev reddede; de blev fundne, drivende om paa en Mast, *a lady and her child were rescued; they were found drifting about on a mast.*

de øvrige druknede allesammen; hvis et Skib havde været nær, kunde de alle være blevet reddede, *the rest were all drowned; if a ship had been near, they might all have been saved.*

tag dig iagt, Nils, eller du bliver overkjørt! *Take care, Nils, or you will be run over.*

vi bliver trykket fordærvet allesammen, hvis vi ikke snart kommer ud, *we shall all be squeezed to death if we don't get out soon.*

jeg vilde være blevet trykket fordærvet, hvis vi ikke var komne ud, *I should have been squeezed to death if we had not got out.*

vi vilde have været i Trondhjem nu, hvis du ikke var kommen for sent til Toget, *we should have been at Trondhjem by this time if you had not been too late for the train.*

Tyvene vilde være blevet grebne, hvis de var blevet forfulgte strax, *the thieves would have been taken if they had been followed at once.*

'Fy! skamme dig!' 'Hvad har jeg da gjort?' 'Du har slaaedes i Kirken, og mens Præsten stod og messede.' *'Fie! for shame!' 'Why, what have I done?' 'You were fighting in church, when the priest was standing and intoning the service.'*

en ny Skuespillerinde skulde optræde, *a new actress was going to appear on the stage.*

mellem Publikum hviskedes mangehaande Ting før Tæppet gik op, *many whispered remarks were made among the audience before the curtain drew up.*

hun skulde have været en skrækkelig Jentunge, og, siden som voxen været forlovet med sex Personer paa een Gang, og have holdt det gaaende i et halvt Aar. *She was said to have been a terrible child,* and, since she was grown up, to have been engaged to half a dozen men at the same time, and to have kept it going for six months.

hun skulde være bleven ledsaget ud af Byen af Politivagt, fordi den var i fulstændigt Oprør for hendes Skyld; det var mærkeligt, at Direktionen tillod en saadan Person at træde op. *It was said she had been conducted by the police out of the town, which was in a state of uproar about her; the wonder was the managers allowed such a person to appear on the stage.*

andre paastod, der var ikke mindste Sandhed deri, hun var, fra, hun var ti Aar, opdraget hos en stille Præstefamilie i Bergens Stift: hun var en dannet, elskelig Pige, de kjendte hende godt, hun maatte have et mageløst Talent; thi hun var saa smuk. *Others insisted upon it there was not the least truth in these tales. She had been since the age of ten brought up in a quiet clergyman's family in the Bergen district. She was a respectable, amiable girl, they knew her well, she must have exceptional talent: for she was so pretty!*

Dit Rige komme, *Thy kingdom come.*

helliget vorde dit Navn, *hallowed be Thy name.*

der det var blevet Aften, der Solen var nedgangen, *when it was evening, now that the sun had gone down.*

det hele Korps var nær bleven taget til Fange, *the whole company were nearly taken prisoners.*

et stjaalent Øiekast, *a stolen glance.*

jeg fik ikke andet end Smørrebrød, det lagde jeg paa Ovnen, og Brødet brand, og Smørret rand, og aldrig fik jeg igjen et eneste Gran, *I got nothing else than bread and butter, I laid it on the stove, and the bread burnt, and the butter melted, and I never got the tiniest bit of it again.*

alt Vand siger til Strand, og Penge til den rige Mand, *all wares set toward the land, and all money flows towards the rich man.*

han kunde jaget bort min Hund med nogle Børst, jeg selv da skulde sagt, han gjorde vel, *he might have driven forth my dog with a broom, and I myself would have said he did right.*

det begyndte at blive sent, *it was getting late.*

han blev anseet for en stor Skribent, *he was looked upon as a great writer.*

VERBS.

Auxiliary Verbs.

Note.—Most of the auxiliary verbs can be also used independently.

At være, *to be.*

Indicative Mood.

Present, *am, are*: jeg, du, han er; vi, I, de ere.
Imperfect, *was, were*: sing. var; plur. vare.
Perfect, *have been*: sing. har været; plur. have været.
Pluperfect, *had been*: sing. havde været; plur. havde været.
Future, *will*, or *shall be*: sing. vil, or skal; plur. ville, or skulle være.

Imperative Mood.

Present, *be thou, be ye*: sing. vær; plur. værer.

Optative.

let be, be it, være.

Participle.

Present, *being*, værende.
Past, *been*, været.

Examples.

det var nu kommet dertil, *things had now come to such a pass.*
dersom han ikke var, *if it had not been for him.*
hvis saa er at, *if so be that.*
det er sagt, *it has been said.*
der er dem som, *there are those who.*
det var morsomt, *that is a good joke.*
ingen, være sig Fremmed eller Indfødt, *no one whether (be he) foreigner or native.*
det være nu som det vil, *be that as it may.*
det faar saa være, *so let it be.*
Skibet skulde være [skulde have været], her den Femte, *the ship should [have been] here on the fifth.*
jeg har været hos Dem, *I have called on you.*
de skulde være kommen, *they were supposed to have come.*

At blive, *to be, remain, become.*

Indicative.

Present and Future, *am, shall be*: jeg, du, han, bliver ; vi, I, de blive.
Imperfect, *was, were, became*: jeg, du, han ; vi, I, de blev.

Imperative.

be, bliv.

Participle.

become: bleven; plur. blevne; neut. blevet.

Examples.

bliv her, *stay here*.
han er og bliver en Nar, *he is a fool and ever will be*.
alle blev staaende, *they all continued standing*.
bliv ikke vred, *don't be angry*.
det bliver sent, *it is getting late*.
det bliver, vil blive, vanskeligt, *it will be difficult*.
Gud sagde vorde Lys, og der blev Lys, *God said let there be light and there was light*.
hvor er min Bog bleven af? *what is become of my book?*
dette bliver imellem os, *this is to go no further*.
det blev til Intet, *it came to nothing*.
det blev ikke derved, *the matter did not stop there*.
vi have her ikke en blivende Stad, *we have here no abiding city*.
jeg bliver tyve Aar imorgen, *I shall be twenty to-morrow*.
naar bliver det? *when is it to be?*
han blev stadig ved at gaae, *he kept moving*.

At have, *to have*; *passive*, at haves.

Indicative.

Present, *have*; sing. har; plur. have.
Imperfect, *had*: sing. havde; plur. havde.
Perfect, *have had*: sing. har havt; plur. have havt.
Pluperfect, *had had*: sing. and plur. havde havt.
Future, *shall have*: sing. vil, skal; plur. ville, skulle have.

Imperative.

Present, *have*: sing. hav; plur. have.

VERBS.

PARTICIPLE.

Present, *having*, havende ; Perfect, *had*, havt.

Examples.

der har vi det, *that's it.*
han havde Hatten paa, *he had his hat on.*
det haves ikke her, *it is not to be had here.*

At skulle, *to be about to, to be meant to, to be obliged to.*

INDICATIVE MOOD.

Present, *shall*: sing. jeg, du, han skal ; plur. vi, I, de skulle.
Imperfect, *should*: sing. skulde ; plur. skulde.
Perfect, *have been obliged*: sing. har ; plur. have skullet.

Examples.

du skal (old form, skalt) blive belønnet, *you shall be rewarded.*
det skulde gjøre mig ondt, *I should be sorry for it.*
det skulde jeg mene, *I should think so.*
hvad skal jeg med det ? *what am I to do with it ?*
hvor skal De hen ? *where are you going to ?*
Hunden skal ud, *the dog wants to get out.*
skulde han dø inden den Tid, *if he were to die before then.*
skulde det have været Katten ? *could it have been the cat ?*
hvorledes skulde jeg kunne, *how should I be able ?*
jeg skal ikke kunne sige det, *I can't tell.*
jeg skulde have været der, *I was to have been there.*
der skal mange Penge til at reise til England, *it takes a good deal of money to travel to England.*
han skal være hemmelig gift, *he is said to be privately married.*

At ville, *to be about to, to be willing.*

INDICATIVE.

Present, *will, am, are willing*: sing. jeg, du, han vil ; plur. vi, I, de ville
Imperfect, *would*: jeg, du, vi, &c., vilde.
Perfect, *have been willing*: sing. jeg, du, han har ; vi, I, de have villet;
 Obs. du vilt, *thou wilt*, is also found.

Examples.

jeg har aldrig sagt at jeg skulde ville bo der, *I never said that I should wish to live there.*
vil du som jeg, *if you are of my mind.*
hvad vilde han her? *what did he want here?*
han har villet min Død, *he wished my death.*
jeg vilde just have gaaet da Du kom, *I was just going away when you came.*
jeg vilde gjerne have den Bog, *I should like to have that book.*
man vil have seet ham her, *it is understood that he has been seen here.*
hvad vil Du (have) at jeg skal gjøre? *what will you have me do?*
jeg vil ikke leve længe, *I shall not live long.*
Blod vil frem, *murder will out.*
vil du med? *will you come with us?*

At maatte, *to be obliged*, of general obligation as opposed to faar.

INDICATIVE.

Present, *may, must*: jeg, du, han; vi, I, de maa.
Imperfect, *was, were obliged*: jeg, du, han; vi, I, de maatte.
Perfect, *have been obliged*: jeg, du, han har maattet; vi, I, de have maattet.

Examples.

maa jeg gaa med? *may I go along with you?*
han maa sige hvad han vil, *say what he will.*
maa Ingen af os opleve den Dag, *may none of us live to see that day.*
han bad om at hun maatte blive indladet, *he requested that she might be admitted.*
maa du gaa ud at spadsere? *are you allowed to take a walk?*
jeg maa meget ofte sende ham til Byen, *I am obliged to send him to town very often.*
han maatte gaa, *he had to walk.*
jeg maatte le, *I couldn't help laughing.*
han maatte til, *he had to submit.*

At kunne, *to be able.*

INDICATIVE.

Present, *can*: jeg, du, han kan; vi, I, de kunne.
Imperfect, *could*; jeg, du, han; vi, I, de kunde.

Perfect, *have been able*: sing. jeg, du, han har kunnet; plur. vi, I, de have kunnet.

Future, *shall be able*: jeg, du, han vil, eller, skal kunne; vi, I, de ville, eller, skulle kunne.

Obs. du kansk, *thou canst*, is also found.

Examples.

jeg har kunnet gjøre det da jeg var yngre, *I could do it when I was younger.*
han begynder at kunne læse, *he is beginning to read.*
nu kan det være nok, *that will do.*
de som ikke kan Sproget, *those that are ignorant of the language.*
Gutten kunde sin Lektie, *the boy knew his lesson.*
det kan jeg ikke for, *it is not my fault.*
hvad kan jeg for at hun græder? *how can I help her weeping?*

At burde, *to owe as a duty.*

INDICATIVE.

Present, *ought*: jeg, du, han; vi, I, de bør.
Imperfect, *was in duty bound*: jeg, du, &c., burde.

Examples.

Du bør gjøre det, *you ought to do it.*
som det sig hør og bør, *as is meet and proper.*
det bør enhver at være besindig, *it behoves every one to be discreet.*

At turde, *to dare.*

INDICATIVE.

Present, *dare, may, am allowed*: jeg, du, &c., tør.
Imperfect, *dared, might*: jeg, du, &c., turde.

Examples.

jeg tør nok sige, *I think I may safely say.*
tør jeg spørge Dem, *may I ask you.*
det turde vel hænde sig, *that might possibly happen.*

At faae, *to get, to have, to have to.*

INDICATIVE.

Present, *get*: sing. jeg, du, han faar; plur. vi, I, de faae.
Past, *got*: jeg, du, han; vi, I, de fik.

IMPERATIVE.

get, seize: faa.

PARTICIPLE.

got, gotten: faaet.

Obs. Faa, as opposed to maa, burde, implies obligation in special cases.

Examples.

jeg faar vel have en Mark for Koen, *I must have a mark for the cow.*
jeg har faaet min Frakke repareret, *I have had my coat mended.*
naar jeg faar Bogen læst, *when I shall have read the book.*
jeg faar vel gjøre det, *I suppose I shall have to do it.*
det faar at være, *let that pass.*
det faar være tilladt at, *it must be allowed to.*
det faar gaae som det kan, *that may go as it likes.*
vi faar at see, *we shall see.*
han faar at spise Fisk, *he is allowed to eat fish.*
Du faar blive hjemme, *you must stay at home.*
vi fik ham med, *we made him come.*
han fik dem alle til at le, *he set them all laughing.*

Mon, monne, *doth, did, may, might*, obsolete, poetical, sometimes classed with the Auxiliary Verbs.

hun ser hvordan det monne lade, *she is trying how it doth look.*
de monne sætte sig, *they did sit them down.*

There are also some other words which are quasi-auxiliary, being used occasionally where we use auxiliaries in English; e. g. **Holde paa.**

Du har holdt paa at skrive i hele Dag, *you have been writing all day.*
jeg holdt netop at slutte Brevet, du kom ind, *I was just finishing the letter when you came in.*

Gjøre, with infinitive; as

bedrage gjør han, *he does cheat.*

VERBS.

nei, sælge den gjør jeg ikke, sagde Askeladden, *nay, sell it I will not, said the cinder-boy.*

sørge gjorde hun, *mourn she did.*

with Indicative, in Norwegian; as

flør gjorde han, som han var gal, *flew, he did, as if he was mad.*

han slog et Slag med dem, og drak med dem gjorde han ogsan, *he struck a blow with them, and drank with them he did also.*

CONJUGATION.

There are Three Conjugations.

The First, where the past Indicative ends in **ede**, as jeg elskede, *I loved.*

The Second, where the past Indicative ends in **te**, as jeg hørte, *I heard.*

The Third, where the past Indicative is a **monosyllable**, as jeg gav, *I gave.*

The first and second are also sometimes called WEAK, and sometimes REGULAR Conjugations, and the third IRREGULAR or STRONG.

First Conjugation.

Verbs of the first Conjugation add to the stem **ede** for the past Indicative, and **et** for the past Participle.

Such for the most part are Verbs whose stem ends in t, ndr, ndl; e. g.

	Present Indic.	Past Indic.	Past Part.
I throw	kaster	kastede	kastet
wait	venter	ventede	ventet
fetch	henter	hentede	hentet
work	arbeider	arbeidede	arbeidet
care	agter	agtede	agtet
wander	vandrer	vandrede	vandret

	Present Indic.	Past Indic.	Past Part.
approach	naaer	naaede	naaet
believe	troer	troede	troet
dwell	boer	boede	boet
doubt	tvivler	tvivlede	tvivlet
imprison	fængsler	fængslede	fængslet
trade	handler	handlede	handlet
fish	fiske	fiskede	fisket

Obs. When the stem of the Verb ends in a vowel, the **e** following is mute in pronunciation, and generally omitted in writing, as, **han tror,** *he believes*; **de tro,** *they believe*; **han flyr,** *he flies*; **de naaede,** *they came near* (pron. naadde); but the **e** is retained in the passive, as **han troes,** *he is believed.*

The final **e** of the past indicative is often left out in verse; and in talking **elskede** is pronounced **elsket.**

If the stem, which is also the form of the imperative, ends in a combination of consonants that cannot stand by itself, **e** is added, as **aabne Døren,** *open the door.*

Second Conjugation.

The past indicative ends in **te** or **de**, the past participle in **t**.

To this Conjugation belong Verbs whose stem ends in **mm, ld, nd, ng,** or in a **single consonant.**

	Present Indic.	Past. Indic.	Past Part.
use	bruger	brugte	brugt
think	tænke	tængte	tænkt
feel	føle	følte	følt
forget	glemme	glemte	glemt
call	kalder	kaldte	kaldt
know	kjender	kjendte	kjendt
learn	lærer	lærte	lært
lose	taber	tabte	tabt
say	siger	sagde	sagt

VERBS.

	Present Indic.	Past Indic.	Past Part.
ask	spørger	spurgte	spurgt
mean, think	mener	mente	ment
send	sender	sendte	sendt
praise	roser	roste	rost
have	(haver) har	havde	havt
{ *smoke, e.g.* { *tobacco*	røger	røgte	røgt
{ *prepare by* { *smoking*	røger	røgede	røget
talk	taler	talede	talt
print	trykker	trykte	trykt
weigh down	trykker	trykkede	trykket

Obs. The past participle of weak Verbs had originally two forms, one ending in **d** for the common gender, and one in **t** for the neuter, as **elsked, elsket.** The form in **d** is now obsolete.

At gjøre, *to do,* makes **gjør,** *I do, thou dost, he does,* in the ind. pres. sing.

At spørge, makes **spør,** *I, you, he, &c., ask.*

At have, makes **har** for ind. pres. sing. and plur.

At vide, *to know;* **han veed,** *I, thou, he, knows;* **vide,** *we, you, they know;* **du veedst,** *thou knowest,* also occurs.

Past ind., **vidste**; past part., **vidst.**

Imperative, **vid,** *know thou;* **vider,** *know ye.*

Some Verbs of this Conjugation change the vowel in the past indicative and past participle, generally **æ** into **a** and **o** into **u.**

	Present Indic.	Past Indic.	Past Part.
set, place	sætter	satte	sat
rouse, excite	vækker	vakte	vakt
awaken from sleep		vækkede	vækket
choke	kvæler	kvalte	kvalt
choose	vælger	valgte	valgt
count	tæller	talte	talt
reach	rækker (intr.)	rakte	ragt

	Present Indic.	Past Indic.	Past Part.
stretch	strækker	strakte	strakt
accustom	vænner	vante	vant
bring	bringer	bragte	bragt
conceal	dølger	dulgte	dulgt
follow	følger	fulgte	fulgt
ask	spørger	spurgte	spurgt
smear	smører	smurte	smurt
sell	sælger	solgte	solgt
tread	træder	traadte	traadt
lay	lægge	lagde	lagt
say	siger	sagde	sagt
do	gjør	gjorde	gjort

Third Conjugation.

To this Conjugation belong the so called Strong Verbs.

The past indicative is formed without adding any termination by changing the stem vowel of the present, as **jeg tager, jeg tog**; *I take, I took*.

The past participle, with or without change of the stem vowel, ends in **et** or **t** for the neuter, and in most cases in **en** for the common gender; plural **ne**; as

binder, *bind*, bandt, bundet, -en, -ne (see ante, p. 61).

Obs. In the spoken language the past part. always ends in **et** or **t**, with the auxiliary Verbs **være** and **blive**, as well as with **have** and **faa**.

Some Verbs of this Conjugation in which the stem vowel is long distinguish in the written language the plural from the singular in the past indicat. as **jeg skrev, vi skreve**, *I wrote, we wrote*, from **skriver**. This distinction is not observed in speaking.

The plural termination **e** is omitted, (α) when the stem-vowel in the present tense is short, as **jeg springer, vi sprang**; (β) where the past and present have the same vowel, as **vi græde**, *we weep*, **vi græd**, *we wept*; (γ) where the past ends in a vowel, as **vi lo**, *we laughed*, **de fløi**, *they flew*, also, **de krøb**, *they crept*.

VERBS. 79

Many strong Verbs lack the past part. in en, as **seet**, *seen*; **bidt**, *bitten*; and some have two forms, as **slagen, slaaet,** *smitten*; sometimes with a somewhat different application, as **svinge svang, svunget** and **svingede svinget**; hun svingede med Lommetørklædet, *she waved her pocket-handkerchief*; han svang sig i Sadelen, *he vaulted into the saddle.* So in English we say, *the man was hanged, the clothes were hung up.*

Verbs of the **Third Conjugation** are divided into SIX CLASSES according to the change of vowel in the past indicative and past participle.

First Class.

	i	a	u		
				Past Part.	
	Present Indic.	Past Indic.	neut.	com.	pl
bind	binder	bandt	bundet	en	ne
find	finder	fandt	fundet	en	ne
spin	spinder	spandt	spundet	en	ne
vanish	svinder	svandt	svundet	en	ne
twine	tvinder	tvandt	tvundet	en	ne
leap	springer	sprang	sprunget	en	ne
swing	svinger	svang	svunget	en	ne
constrain	tvinger	tvang	tvunget	en	ne
burst	brister	brast	brustet	en	ne
let slip, slip	slipper	slap	sluppet	en	ne
drink	drikker	drak	drukket	en	ne
prick	stikker	stak	stukket	en	ne
	(stinger	stang	stunget	en	ne)
	y	a	u		
sing	synger	sang	sunget	en	ne
sink	synker	sank	sunket	en	ne
	æ	a	u		
break	brækker	brak	brukket	en	ne
hit upon	træffer	traf	truffet	en	ne
help	hjælpe	hjalp	hjulpet	en	ne

Second Class.

i, e, æ, a		a	a, aa, or, the Vowel of the Present.		
	Present Indic.	Past Indic.	neut.	com.	pl.
give	giver	gav	givet	en	ne
feel inclined to	gider	gad	gidet		
sit	sidder	sad	siddet		
lie	ligger	laa	ligget		
beg	beder	bad	bedet bedt		
see	seer	saa	seet		
feed upon	æder	aad	ædt		
am	er	var	været		
be worth	gjælder	gjaldt	gjældt		
tremble	skjælver	skjalv	sjælvet		
reach	rækker (tran.)	rak	rakt rukket		
stretch	strækker (intr.)	strak	strakt		
hang	hænger (intr.)	hang	hængt		
bear	bærer (bær)	bar	baaret	en	ne
cut	skjærer (skjær)	skar	skaaret	en	ne
steal	stjæler	stjal	stjaalet	en	ne

Third Class.

	i long	e	e and i		
be, become	bliver	blev	blevet	en	ne
snatch	griber	greb	grebet	en	ne
slide	glider	gled	gledet	en	ne
pipe	piber	peb	pebet		
rub	gnider	gned	gnedet	en	ne
grind	sliber	sleb	slebet	en	ne
pinch	kniber	kneb	knebet	en	ne
ride	rider	red	redet	en	ne
drive	driver	drev	drevet	en	ne
write	skriver	skrev	skrevet	en	ne
screech	skriger	skreg	skreget		
sneak	sniger	sneg	sneget		
mount	stiger	steg	steget	en	ne
deceive	sviger	sveg	sveget	en	ne
bite	bider	bed	bidt		
suffer	lider	led	lidt		

VERBS.

	Præs. Indic.	Past. Indic.	Past. Part. neut.	com.	plur.
tear	slider	sled	slidt		
pitch	smider	smed	smidt		
fight	strider	stred	stridt		
twist	vrider	vred	vredet	en	ne

Fourth Class.

	y	ø	u, ø, y, o		
break, trouble	bryder	brød	brudt		
bid, order	byder	bød	budt	en	ne
shoot	skyder	skjød	skudt		
flow	flyder	flød	flydt		
pour out	gyder	gjød	gydt		
sound	lyder	lød	lydt		
enjoy	nyder	nød	nydt		
sneeze	nyser	nøs	nyst		
creep	kryber	krøb	krøbet	en	ne
stroke, smooth	stryger	strøg	strøget	en	ne
climb	klyver	kløv	kløvet		
fly	flyver	fløi	fløiet	en	ne
tell a lie	lyver	løi	løiet		
freeze	fryser	frøs	frosset	en	ne

Fifth Class.

	a, aa, æ, e	o	a, o, e		
draw, march	drager	drog	draget	en	ne
hunt	jager	jog, jagede	jaget		
fare, travel	farer	foer	faret	en	ne
let	lader	lod	ladet		
take	tager	tog	taget	en	ne
smile	slaar	slog	slaaet		
			slagen		ne
stand	staar	stod	staaet		
	(stander)		standen, in comp.		
swear	sværger	svor	svoret	en	ne
laugh	ler	lo	leet		
command	befaler	befol	befol		
		befalede	befalet		

G

Obs. **drager, tager, sværger**, are pronounced drar, tar, svær.
The old Imperat. of **staar** is **stat,** *stand!*

Sixth Class.

Verbs that have the same vowel in the present, past, and past participle.

run	løber	løb	løbet,	en	ne
sleep	sover	sov	sovet		
weep	græder	græd	grædt		
am called	heder	hed, hedte	hedt		
hew	hugger	hug	huggen		
		huggede	hugget		
come	kommer	kom	kommet	en	ne
fall	falder	faldt	faldt	en	ne
hold	holder	holdt	holdt		

Anomalous:

jeg faar, *I get*; fik, *got*; faaet, *gotten.*
jeg gaaer, *I go*; gik, *went*; gaaet, *gone.*
han fanger, *he catches*; vi finge, *we caught.*
han ganger, *he goes*; de ginge, *they went*; gak, *go thou.*

Deponent Verbs.

There are certain Verbs which have only the passive form; e. g.

at blues, *to be ashamed.* at længes, *to long for.* at ældes, *to grow old.* at lykkes, *to succeed* or *befal.* at undres, *to be astonished.* at mindes, *to recollect.*

Some of these have a reciprocal meaning; as

at kives, *to wrangle.* at kappes, *to vie with.* at enes, *to agree.* at slaaes, *to fight.*

Deponent Verbs have a past part., identical in form with the

1st indic. in **es**, which is used in the compound tenses after an auxiliary Verb; e.g.

    jeg har længtes, *I have longed for.*　　det er lykkedes mig, *it has happened to me.*

But some other form of expression is often substituted for this; e.g. instead of **de har enedes**, *or* **enets**, they say, **de er levne**, or **blevet** (pron. **blet**), **enige**, *they have come to an agreement.*

The following are among the commonest of the Deponent Verbs:—

	Pres.	Past Indic. and Part.
be at one with	enes	enedes, enedes
long for	længes	længtes
happen to	lykkes	lykkedes, lyktes
recollect	mindes	mindedes
wonder	undres	undredes
pity	ynkes	ynkedes

lykkes, in the sense of *succeed*, is used impersonally:—
    det lykkedes ham, *he succeeded.*

undres is also used reflexively:—
    jeg undrede mig, *or*, jeg undredes, *I wondered, I was astonished.*

REFLEXIVE VERBS.

Reflexive Verbs, which are not much used in English, are common in Norsk. They are those Verbs which have for their object the same person as the subject (for the 3rd pers. the reflexive Pronoun **sig**); e.g.

  jeg skammer mig, *I am ashamed.*　　vi skamme os, *we are ashamed.*
  du skammer dig, *thou art ashamed.*　I skamme eder, Jer, *ye are ashamed.*
  han skammer sig, *he is ashamed.*　　de skamme sig, *they are ashamed.*

The following Verbs are used reflexively in Norsk, where in English the Verb is intransitive:—

at aabne sig, *to open.*
at bøie sig, *to bend.*
at bevæge sig, *to move.*
at forandre sig, *to change.*
at føle sig, *to feel*, e. g. *better.*
at klæde sig, *to dress.*
at læne sig, *to lean.*
at røre sig, *to move.*
at samle sig, *to assemble.*
at vende sig, *to turn.*

In some Verbs the meaning is modified when they are used reflexively; as

forestille, *to present*; forestille sig, *to figure to oneself.*
indbilde, *to make one believe*; indbilde sig, *to delude oneself into the belief.*
komme, *to come*; komme sig, *to recover, come to oneself.*
opføre, *to raise*; opføre sig, *to conduct oneself.*

Some are used only as reflexive; as

forstille sig, *to dissemble.*
forkjøle sig, *to catch cold.*
vægre sig, *to refuse, decline to do.*

Impersonal Verbs.

Some are only used with **det** as subject; as

det regner, *it rains.* det tordner, *it thunders.* det lyner, *it lightens.*
det dages, *it dawns.* det vaares, *spring is coming.*

Others can take a definite subject, but only in the third person; as

en Ulykke hændte, *or*, skede, *a mischance happened*, from det sker, det hænder, *it happens.*

Some Intransitive Verbs are used impersonally in the passive form, with **der** instead of **det**; as

der dandses, *there is a dance going on.*
der kriges, *there is war.*
der spilles, *they are playing.*
der iles, *they are in a hurry.*
der siges, *people say.*
der er dem som, *there are those who.*
der gives dem som, *there are those who.*
der findes dem som, *people are found who.*

Examples.

det synes mig, *it seems to me.*
jeg synes, *methinks.*
som De synes, *as you please.*
hvad synes De derom? *what do you think of it?*
det banker, *there is a knock at the door.*
det blev ringet paa Klokken, *there was a ring at the bell.*
det blev mig fortalt, *I was informed.*
det glæder mig, *I am glad.*
der dansedes og spilledes, *there was dancing and music.*
det lykkedes ham at gjenvinde Pengene, *he succeeded in getting back the money.*
hvem er den Gut? det er min Broder, *who is that boy? He (it) is my brother.*
hvem er disse Piger? det er Kapteinens Døttre, *who are those girls? They are (it is) the captain's daughters.*
jeg skulde have Lyst at reise med, men der er ikke at tale om det, *I should like to go too, but it is out of the question.*
det har regnet hele Ugen, og det kommer til at regne idag ogsaa, er jeg bange for, *it has rained all the week, and I am afraid it is going to rain to-day too.*
ved du, hvilken By der er den største i Norge næst Christiana? *do you know which (there) is the largest town in Norway next to Christiana?*
hun synes om at bo i Byen, men vi synes bedre om Landet, *she likes to live in town, but we like the country better.*

ADVERBS.

Formation of Adverbs.

Most Adjectives may be used adverbially. Those that end in **ig, lig**, mostly retain the termination of the common gender; as ærlig, Adject. *honest*, Adv. *honestly*.

The others are used as Adverbs in the neuter gender; as langsomt, *slowly*.

Some end in **e**; as ofte, *often*; bare, *only*.

Some add **lig**; as nylig, *recently*; sandelig, *truly*; daglig, *daily*.

Some add **viis**; as muligviis, *possibly*; heldigviis, *fortunately*; deelviis, *partly*.

Some Adverbs are compounded e. g. of a Preposition and a Substantive; as

> tilsengs, *to bed*; tilstede, *at hand*; idag, *to-day*; iblinde, *in the dark*; efterhaanden, *by degrees;* undertiden, *sometimes.*

Or, of other parts of speech; as

> vistnok, *surely*; maaske, *may be*; kanske, *perhaps.*

Adverbs are also formed by the terminations **sinde, lunde, deles**; as

> ingenlunde, *by no means*; særdeles, *especially*; ligeledes, *likewise.*

Participles are used without change as Adverbs; e. g.

> kogende hed, *boiling hot*; udmærket vakker, *remarkably handsome.*

Also the termination **ende** is sometimes added to a Substantive to form an Adverb; as

> kullende sort, *coal-black*; isende kold, *ice-cold.*

From the various kinds of Pronouns are formed Pronominal Adverbs, viz.

ADVERBS.

Demonstrative; as

da, *then*; der, *there*; did, *thither*; dertil, *thereto*; derfra, *therefrom*; derom, *about that*; her, *here*; hid, *hither*; herhen, *this way*; derden, *that way, thither*; heden, *hence*; saa, saaledes, *so*; jo, desto, *by how much, by so much*; jo mere, jo bedre, *the more the better*; thi, *therefore, consequently.*

Interrogative; as

hvor, *where, how?* naar, *when?* hvorledes, *how?* hvorfor, *wherefore?* hvorfra, *wherefrom?* hvorom, *what about?* hvi, *why?*

Relative. The above may also be used as oblique interrogatives and relatives.

Indefinite.

der, as, der er, *there is*; noget, *somewhat*; aldrig, *never*; ingensteds, *nowhere.*

Examples.

Den er ærlig sine ti Kroner værd, *it is honestly worth ten crowns.*
tal høit, *speak loud*,—høiere, *louder.*
kom snarest muligt, *come as soon as possible.*
nu skal du peent opføre dig, *now behave nicely.*
bliv ikke længe! *don't be long!*
han kommer ofte paa dette Sted, *he frequents this place.*
bare hun var her! *if only she were here!*
han vil endelig reise, *he must needs go.*
hun vilde endelig have at jeg skulde trine ind, *she would insist on my stepping in.*
det maa De endelig ikke glemme, *you must be sure not to forget that.*
jeg kommer øieblikkelig, *I will come directly.*
Doktoren kom hurtig tilstede, *the doctor was promptly in attendance.*
Skoene lod sig ikke længere istand sætte, *the shoes would not bear any more mending.*
han er meget rask tilfods, *he is a very good walker.*
afsted med dig, *off with you!*
vistnok maa man erkjende, *it must certainly be admitted.*
kanske han er ikke ædru, *possibly he is not sober.*
aldeles ikke, *decidedly not.*

dersom han er nogenlunde istand dertil, *if he is anything like able to do it.*

Naa, saaledes! *Oh, I see, that's how it is, is it?*

Comparison of Adverbs.

Adverbs that are identical in form with the common or neuter gender of Adjectives, are compared like Adjectives; as

| daarlig, *poor, poorly* | daarligere | daarligst |
| snart, *quick, quickly* | snarere | snarest |

Likewise some that end in **e**; as

| længe, *long* | længere | længst |
| ofte, *frequently* | oftere | oftest |

And the following, which borrow the comparative and superlative from a different stem:—

vel, *well*	bedre	bedst
ilde, *ill*	værre	værst
gjerne, *gladly*	hellere	helst
	heller	
meget, *much*	mere	mest
lidt, *little*	mindre	mindst

Other Adverbs, not admitting of inflexion, are compared by the help of **mere, mest**.

Examples.

han stod tidlig op, *he got up early.*

Damskibet kommer ikke tidligere end Klokken fem, *the steamer does not come earlier than 5 o'clock.*

han har snarere vundet end tabt i Styrke, *he has rather gained than lost in strength.*

hun skriver lettere Engelsk end Norsk, *she writes English more easily than Norse.*

det er ikke længere siden end igaar, *it was only yesterday.*

aldrig oftere, *never again.*

vi maa hellere gaa, *we had better go.*

snarest muligt, *as soon as possible.*

ADVERBS.

The following are the most important Adverbs, classified according to signification:—

TEMPORAL ADVERBS.

da, *then*
endnu, *yet*
nu, *now*
aldrig, *never*
altid, *always*
allerede, *already*
atter, *again*
igjen, *again*
derpaa, *thereupon*
engang, *once*
fordum, *formerly*
før, *before, till*
hyppig, *frequently*
tidt, *often*
ofte, *often*
idag, *to-day*
iaften, *this evening*
inat, *to-night, last night*
imorgen, *to-morrow*

imorges, *this morning*
imorgen tidlig, *to-morrow morning*
iovermorgen, *the day after to-morrow*
igaar, *yesterday*
igaar aftes, *last evening*
iforgaars, *the day before yesterday*
idag otte Dage, *a week hence*
næste Uge, *next week*
ifjor, *last year*
itide, *in time*
just nu, *just now*
seent, *late*
snart, *soon*
straks, *directly*
siden, *since*
naar, *when*
sjelden, *seldom*
sildig, *late*
undertiden, *sometimes*

Examples.

om han havde aldrig saa mange, *though he had ever so many.*
dette kan vel aldrig være Deres Klæder? *these are never surely your clothes?*
Enden er ikke endnu, *the end is not yet.*
ikke saa gal endnu, *not so bad after all.*
allerede dengang, *even at that time.*
atter andre, *others still.*
kommer du endelig engang, *here you are at last.*
før vil jeg sulte, *I will starve first.*
jo før jo heller, *the sooner the better.*
sent ere bedre end aldrig, *better late than never.*
De kommer for sent, *you are too late.*

Klokken er strax tolv, *it is close upon twelve.*
strax da jeg saae det, *the moment I saw it.*
sjelden eller aldrig, *rarely if ever.*

Local Adverbs.

der, *there*	nedenunder, *downstairs*
did, *thither*	ovenpaa, *upstairs*
her, *here*	overalt, *everywhere*
hid, *hither*	tilbage, *back*
hen, *hence*	udenfor, *outside*
hvor, *where*	nordenfor, *North of*
langt, *far*	østenfor, *East of*
forbi, *past*	tilstede, *on the spot*

From some Adverbs of place denoting motion new Adverbs implying rest are formed by adding e; as

at gaa bort, *to go away*	at være borte, *to be away*
at komme ind, *to come in*	at være inde, *to be in*
ned, *down*	nede, *down*
op, *up*	oppe, *up*
ud, *out*	ude, *out*
frem, *abroad*	fremme, *abroad*
hen, *away*	henne, *away*
hjem, *home*	hjemme, *at home*

Examples.

det er forbi med ham, *it is all over with him.*
det være langt fra mig, *far be it from me.*
han boer ovenpaa, *he lives up above.*
det bruges overalt i Verden, *it is used in all parts of the world.*
hvem staar udenfor Døren? *who stands before the door?*
Herr Nielssen er inde, kom du ind, *Mr. Nielsen is within, come in.*
De maa gaae op til Værelset, Deres Ven er ikke oppe endnu, *you must go up to the room, your friend is not up yet.*
ude af Øie er ude af Sind, *out of sight is out of mind.*
dette Svar bragte ham ud af sig selv, *this answer made him beside himself.*
frem med Jer, *out with you.*
der er langt frem, *we have a long way before us.*

ADVERBS.

men nu ere vi snart fremme, *but we shall soon be there.*
jeg veed ikke hvor han er henne, han gik hen igaar, men hvor skal du hen? *I don't know where he is, he went away yesterday, but when are you going?*
han er reist bort, men han bliver ikke længe borte, *he has gone away, but he will not be away long.*

Modal Adverbs.

Saa, saaledes, *so*; hvor, hvorledes, *how*; vel, *well*; ilde, *ill*; galt, *badly*; sagte, *slowly*.

Adverbs of Degree.

Alt for, *too much*; meget, *very*; ganske, *quite*; absolut, *absolutely*; akkurat, *exactly*; overmaade, *excessively*; udmærket, *remarkably*; til, *in addition*—et Glas til, *another glass*; endog, *even*; netop, *just*; neppe, *hardly*; især, *especially*; kun, *only*; blot, *only*; bare, *only*; nok, *enough*; svært, *very*.

Affirmative.

visselig, *certainly*	godt, *very good*
sandelig, *surely*	ja, *yes*
forvist, *for certain*	jo, *yes*
forsand, *of a truth*	

Obs. ja implies entire assent. jo implies more or less of contradiction and correction.

jo is strictly adverbial in the following usages only:—
det er jo saa, *that is certainly the case.*
han er jo streng men ikke urimelig, *he is certainly severe but not unreasonable.*
jeg vil ikke negte at du jo har Ret, *I will not deny that you are right.*
jo senere jo bedre, *the later the better.* (See also pp. 105 below.)

Negative.

ikke, *not*	ei heller, *nor . . . neither*
ei, *not*	langt fra, *far from it*
heller ikke, *nor yet*	Nei, *no*

PREPOSITIONS.

Prepositions in Norse, as in English, generally govern the accusative case, as is seen when an inflected Pronoun follows a Preposition; e. g.

>der er Brev til ham, *there is a letter for him.*

In some few phrases they are followed by the genitive; as

>jeg skal til Sengs, *I shall go to bed.*
>til Bunds, *to the bottom.*
>i Mandags, *last Monday.*

Prepositions are extensively used in composition with Verbs, but are frequently disjoined from their Verb, and placed last in the sentences; as

>Brevet kom ikke rigtig frem, *the letter miscarried.*
>han har intet at leve af, *he has nothing to live upon.*
>det kommer an paa, *that depends.*

Many Prepositions, instead of taking the appropriate Pronouns after them, are compounded with the adverb **der**, and so become Adverbs; as

>deraf, *thereof*, instead of af det, *of it*; dermed, *therewith*; derfor, *therefore*; derom, *concerning that.*

The following are among the most important Prepositions:—

Ad, *towards*, often supplemented by an Adverb; as

>hen ad Veien, *along the road.*
>ned ad Trappen, *down the stairs.*
>jeg reiser ad Bergen til, *I shall travel Bergen way.*

Af, *of, off, from.*

>jeg kjender ham af Navn, *I know him by name.*
>af mange Grunde, *for many reasons.*
>to af dem, *two of them.*
>ved Hjælp af, *by means of.*
>bygget af Træ, *made of wood.*

Kongen af Danmark, *the king of Denmark.*
at hjælpe En af Hesten, *to help one to dismount.*
langt af Veien, *far out of the way.*
af ganske Hjerte, *with all my heart.*
fra Barn af, *from childhood.*
af med Hattene! *hats off!*

An, *on, to,* only in composition and with Verbs.

hvad angaar det mig? *what is that to me?*
det gaar ikke an, *it wont do.*

Bag, *behind.*

bag Døren, *behind the door.*

Efter, *after.*

den Ene efter den Anden, *one after the other.*
han hed Sigurd efter sin Fader, *he was called Sigurd after his father.*
efter hvad jeg har hørt, *after what I have heard.*
efter min Mening, *in my opinion.*
hun slog Døren i efter ham, *she slammed the door after him.*

For, *for, before, to, of, in, by.*

ikke for alt i Verden, *not for the world.*
hvor meget skal De have for det? *how much do you charge for it?*
lige for mig, *straight before me.*
det er det samme for mig, *it is all the same to me.*
at blive fri for, *to get rid of.*
for Alvor, *in earnest.*
han bor for sig, *he lives by himself.*
jeg er ikke meget for det, *I don't much like it.*

In Composition.

Smerten forgaar med Tiden, *the pain will wear off.*
han har forholdt sig meget forsigtig, *he has behaved very prudently.*
det forstaar sig af sig selv, *that is a matter of course.*
Obs. For, used as an Adverb, means *too.* As a Conjunction, *for.*

Fra, *from.*

fra den Tid, *from that time.*
han er fra Trondhjem, *he comes from Trondheim.*

her skilles vi fra hinanden, *here we part.*
det gjør hverken fra eller til, *that is neither here nor there.*

In Composition.

de Fraværende have altid Uret, *the absent are always in the wrong.*

För, *before, prior to.*

Hos, *by, with, at the house of.*

at sidde hos En, *to sit by one.*
Tyven har Uhret hos sig, *the thief has the watch about him.*
han overnattede hos Mølleren, *he put up for the night at the miller's.*

I, *in, to.*

han havde aldrig været i en Kirke, *he had never been in a church.*
god i sit Slags, *good of its kind.*
sende et Barn i Skole, *to send a child to school.*
han har været borte i fem Maaneder, *he has been away five months.*
der sad to Fugle i et Træ, *there sat two birds on a tree.*
han gik ind i Huset, *he went into the house.*
man faar meget at rydde op i, *one finds plenty to settle up in respect of.*

In Composition.

istand, *in order.* istedetfor, *instead of.*

Iblandt, *among.*

iblandt hans mere bekjendte Værker, *among his better known works.*

Igjennem, *through.*

hele Dagen igjennem, *all the day through.*

In Composition, **gjennem.**

at gjennemgaae et Lektie med En, *to go over a lesson with one.*
at kaste gjennemborende Blikke paa Een, *to look daggers at one.*

Imod, *against.*

jeg har ikke noget imod at han kommer, *I have no objection to his coming.*
dersom De har ikke noget imod det, *if you have no objection.*
jeg har intet derimod, *I have no objection.*
vædde ti imod een, *to bet ten to one.*

In Composition.

i Modgangs Skole, *in the school of adversity.*
at høre Grunde og Modgrunde, *to hear arguments for and against.*

Imellem, *between.*

imellem os sagt, *between you and me.*
der er kommet dem noget imellem, *they have had some disagreement.*

In Composition, mellem.

de To døde med faa Dages mellemrum, *the two died within a few days of each other.*

Med, *with.*

med Deres Tilladelse, *with your permission.*
det bliver bedre med ham, *he is better.*
med alt det, *for all that.*
at bære sig galt ad med noget, *to go to work with in the wrong way.*
han er vanskelig at omgaaes med, *he is hard to manage.*
med det Gode eller Onde, *by fair means or foul.*
at holde vaagent Øie med En, *to keep a watchful eye upon one.*
med Eet, *at once.*
han var med de Første, *he was among the first.*

In Composition.

Bogen blev slemt medtagen af Kritikerne, *the book was roughly handled by the critics.*
Skibet kan medtage to hundrede passagerer, *the ship will accommodate 200 passengers.*
hun giver ham Medhold i alt hvad han gjør, *she approves of whatever he does.*

Om, *about.*

hvad mener Du om denne Sag? *what do you think of this matter?*
vi spiller ikke om Penge, *we are not playing for money.*
hun kastede sig om hans Hals, *she fell on his neck.*
det maa hun om, *that's her affair.*
være lang om at klæde sig paa, *to be long over dressing.*
Dør om Dør med, *next door to.*
Posten kommer om Mandagen og Fredagen, *the mail arrives on Mondays and Fridays.*

Om Eftermiddagen, *in the afternoon.*
Om en Time, *in another hour.*
ti Kroner om Ugen, *10 crowns a week.*

In Composition.

sig mig hvem Du omgaar og jeg skal sige Dig hvem Du er, *tell me with whom thou goest and I will tell thee what thou doest.*
det kommer an paa Omstændighederne, *that depends upon circumstances.*

Obs. Om used as a Conjunction = *whether, if.*

Over, *over.*

over hele Byen, *over all the town.*
han sprang over Grøften, *he jumped over the ditch.*
tusinde Fod over Havet, *a thousand feet above the sea.*
jeg saa ham gaa over Gaden, *I saw him go across the street.*
han er noget over femti Aar gammel, *he is something over 50 years old.*
det gaar over min Forstand, *that is beyond my reach.*
Klokken er over To, *it is past two o'clock.*
at tage en grusom Hevn over En, *to take a cruel revenge upon one.*
at sove over sig, *to oversleep oneself.*
over al den Snak glemte jeg at bringe Bogen med, *owing to all that talk I forgot to bring the book with me.*
over det tog han sin Død, *that was the death of him.*
Naturen gaar over Optugtelsen, *Nature is stronger than education.*
jeg gider ikke være over det, *I don't want to be bothered with it.*

In Composition.

jeg overgiver mig i Guds Haand, *I resign myself into the hand of God.*
det Ord har jeg overhørt, *I did not catch that word.*
kan De overlade mig et Pen? *can you spare me a pen?*
jeg overlader til Dem at gjøre Slutningen, *I leave it to you to draw the conclusion.*
at oversætte fra Norsk til Engelsk, *to translate from Norsk into English.*

Obs. As Adverb oven = *above*; as, ovenpaa, *upstairs.*

Paa, *upon, on.*

paa Bordet, *upon the table.*

paa den Betingelse at han skulde betale fem og tyve Specier, *on condition that he should pay 25 dollars.*
paa Søndag, *on Sunday next.*
han bor paa Torvet, *he lives in the market-place.*
paa Landet, paa Marken, paa Engen, *in the country.*
paa min Tid, *in my time.*
han kan gjøre det færdigt paa to Dage, *he can finish it in two days.*
paa Engelsk, *in English.*
han har et Hul paa sin Kjole, *he has a hole in his coat.*
drage ud paa Landet, *to set out for the country.*
paa Theatret, *at the theatre.*
at kjøbe paa anden Haand, *to buy at second hand.*
Svar paa et Brev, *answer to a letter.*
jeg drikker paa Deres lykkelige Reise, *I drink to your prosperous journey.*
sæt det paa min Regning, *set it down to my account.*
han pleier at sove paa Maden, *he is wont to sleep after meals.*
har du Penge paa Dig? *have you any money about you?*
jeg kjender det paa et hemmeligt Mærke, *I know it by a private mark.*
han har forandret sig meget paa nogle Aar, *he has changed a good deal within these last few years.*
at være paa Jagt paa Fjeldet, *to be hunting out on the fells.*
der kommer ti Kroner paa hver, *it comes to ten crowns a head.*
en Kone paa fem og tredive Aar, *a woman of five-and-thirty.*

In Composition.

der paakom mig en heftig Nysen, *I was seized with a fit of sneezing.*
det er paatænkt at bygge en Bro over Floden, *it is intended to build a bridge over the river.*

Til, *to.*

at indbyde til Frokost, *to ask to breakfast.*
at sende Bud til En, *to send a message to one.*
at tage til Bens, *to take to one's heels.*
han gik ad Byen til, *he went towards the town.*
Veien dreier af til Floden, *the road turns off towards the river.*
ti Kroner vil ikke beslaa langt til at betale, *ten crowns will not go far towards paying.*
vent til imorgen, *wait till to-morrow.*

H

han har kjøbt en Bog til mig, *he has bought me a book.*
hvad faa vi til Frokost? *what have we got for breakfast?*
for stor til hende, *too large for her.*
her til Lands, *in this country.*
til Erindring om, *in remembrance of.*
til Hest, *on horseback.*
tilfods, *on foot.*
tilskibs, *on ship board.*
at være til Bryllup, *to be at a wedding.*
hun satte sig hen til ham, *she went and sat down beside him.*
at byde til Gjæst, *to invite as a guest.*
en halv gang til saa lang, *half as long again.*
giv mig Ost at spise til Brødet, *give me some cheese to eat with the bread.*
at see ind til En, *to look in upon one.*

In Composition.

der er intet andet tilbage for ham, *there is nothing else left for him.*
han har tilbragt tre Aar dermed, *he has spent three years upon it.*
i værste Tilfælde, *if the worst comes to the worst.*
du har den Fornøielse tilgode, *you have that pleasure to come.*
tillad mig at bemærke, *allow me to observe.*
han har ingen Penge til overs men han mangler heller ikke Penge, *he has no money to spare, but he doesn't want money either.*
jeg kan aldrig gjøre ham noget tilpas, *I can never do anything to please him.*
jeg tilstaar at jeg ikke før indsaa det rigtige deri, *I own I did not see the truth of it before.*
en saadan Ondskab kunde jeg ikke tiltro ham, *I could never have suspected him of such malice.*

Trods, *in spite of.*

trods den ny Molo var Skib drevne løs paa Haven, *in spite of the new pier ships were driven loose in the harbour.*
trods den Bedste, *as well as the best.*

Uden, *without.*

uden nogen Aarsag, *without any reason.*
jeg kan nok leve uden det, *I dare say I can get on without it.*

Under, *under*.

træde under Fodder, *to tread under foot.*
under tyve Aar, *under 20 years.*
under Laas og Lukke, *under lock and key.*
under disse Omstændigheder, *under these circumstances.*
vi trak ham frem under Sengen, *we dragged him from under the bed.*
han har giftet sig under sin Stand, *he has married beneath him.*
under Krigen, *during the war.*

In Composition.

i Kvinder værer Eders Ægtemænd underdanige, *ye wives, be subject to your own husbands.*

Ved, *by, near to.*

han stod tæt ved Ilden, *he was standing close to the fire.*
han holdt sig fast ved mig, *he held on tight by me.*
ved hans Hjælp, *by his help.*
ved min Ære, *upon my honour.*
Professor ved et Universitet, *professor at a University.*
et Hotel ved en Sø i Italien, *an hotel on an Italian lake.*
jeg fik det at vide ved ham, *I came to know it through him.*
være god ved En, *to be good to one.*
tænke ved sig selv, *to think to oneself.*
der er intet ved ham, *he is not good for much.*
jeg kunde ikke gjøre ved det, *I could not help it.*

In Composition.

jeg har talt med Vedkommenden, *I have spoken with the party concerned.*
de vedblev at være Venner, *they continued to be friends.*
Beslutningen vedtoges enstemmig, *the resolution was carried unanimously.*

CONJUNCTIONS.

The principal CO-ORDINATE CONJUNCTIONS are—

Copulative.

Og, *and, also.*

 og han traadte ind i Skibet, og foer over og kom til sin egen Stad, *and he went into the ship and crossed over and came to his own city.*

 Simon, hvilken han og kaldte Petrus, *Simon whom he also called Peter.*

Samt, *and at the same time.*

Baade—og, *both—and.*

Saavel—som, *as well—as.*

Disjunctive.

Eller, *or.*

 enten han eller jeg, *either he or I.*
 hverken han eller jeg, *neither he nor I.*

Heller ikke, *nor.*

 I er ikke den første Bogbinder, og bliver heller ikke den sidste, der har spoleret en smuk Ryg med en gal Titel, *you are not the first bookbinder, nor will you be the last, that has spoilt a pretty cover with a bad title.*

Adversative.

Men, *but.*

 de Karske have ikke Læge Behov, men de som have Ondt, *the whole need not a physician, but they that are sick.*

Causal.

Thi, *for, because.*

 han er vel værd at du gjør ham dette, thi han elsker vort Folk, *he well deserves that you should do him this service, for he loves our people.*

CONJUNCTIONS. 101

The principal SUBORDINATE CONJUNCTIONS are—

Temporal.

Da, *when, seeing that, since.*

    da han endnu ikke var født, havde jeg allerede staaet tre Gange skoleret, *when he was not yet born I had been three times flogged at school.*

Naar, *when.*

    naar Øllet gaar ind, da gaar Viddet ud, *when the wine is in the wit is out.*

    naar han taler taler han godt, *when he does talk he talks well.*

Efterat, *after that.*

    efterat vi havde spist, *or,* efter at have spist, droge vi afsted, *after we had eaten we departed.*

Før, førend, *before.*

    jeg tror det ikke førend jeg seer det, *I wont believe it before I see it.*

Inden, *before.*

    inden jeg reiser, *before leaving.*

Medens, imedens, *whilst.*

    De maa spise Maden medens den er varm, *you must eat the victuals while hot.*

Indtil, til, *until.*

    Barn skal krybe til det nemmer at gaae, *a child must crawl till it learns to walk.*

Fra, *since.*

    fra jeg var ti Aar gammel, *since I was ten years old.*

Siden, *since.*

    siden han reiste har man intet hørt til ham, *nothing has been heard of him since he went away.*

Som, *as.*

    som jeg staar og tænkede paa Ingenting, faar jeg et Slag over Ryggen. *as I stood thinking about nothing, I felt a slap on the back.*

Saalænge som, *as long as.* Saasnartsom, *as soon as.*

Retsom, *just as.*

  retsom jeg vilde til at skyde, *just as I was going to shoot.*

Allerbedst som, *at the moment that.* Bedst som, *just as.*

  bedst som han skrev, *in the middle of his writing.*

Causal.

Fordi, *because.*

  jeg drikker ikkun Vand fordi jeg taaler ikke at drikke Viin, *I drink nothing but water, because wine does not agree with me.*

Da, *seeing that.*

  Knud mærkede der var noget paafærde, og da han intet forunderligt saa foran sig, vendte han sig om, *Knut perceived there was something the matter, and, inasmuch as he saw nothing remarkable in front of him, he turned round.*

Efterdi, eftersom, *inasmuch as.*

Siden, *since.*

  siden du har gjort mig saa mange Tjenester saa vil du sagtens gjøre mig en til, *since you have done me so many services, you will, I dare say, do me one more.*

Saasom, *since.*

  saa træt som jeg nu er kan jeg intet gjøre, *since I am so tired,* or, *so tired as I now am, I can do nothing.*

Conditional.

Dersom, *in case, if.*

  dersom jeg ikkun faaer rørt ved hans Klædebøn, da bliver jeg helbredet, *if I can only touch the hem of his garment I shall be healed.*

Hvis, *if.*

  jeg vilde have hjulpet dig hvis jeg havde kunnet, *I would have helped you if I had been able.*

Saafremt, *provided that.* Forsaavidt, *in so much as.*

CONJUNCTIONS.

Naar, *if.*
   naar jeg nu gjorde det, hvad blev da Følgen, *suppose I were to do it what would be the consequence?*

Om, *if.*
   om jeg minder ret saa har jeg seet dit Ansigt før, *if I remember rightly I have seen your face before.*
   hvem veed om ikke? *who knows but?*

Medmindre, hvis ikke, *unless.*

Uden, *unless.*
   de ere aldrig fornøiede uden de ere alene, *they are never pleased unless they are alone.*

   Obs. But conditional sentences are very often expressed in Norse, without using the conjunction *if*, the protasis being put in the form of a question; as
   taler han ikke meget, saa tænker han desmere, *if he talks little he thinks all the more.*
   har jeg sagt det, er jeg og Mand for at forsvare det, *if I said it then I am the man to swear to it.*
   kun havde jeg Penge vilde jeg kjøbe det, *I would buy it if I had money.* (See below, p. 39.)

Concessive.

Skjøndt, omendskjøndt, endskjøndt, uagtet, hvorvel, endda, *although*; are used to denote an actual concession; as
   hun lønnes bedre skjøndt jeg har vist mig venligere, *she receives more thanks although I have proved the better friend.*

Om, *although*; **selv om,** *even if*; **om-end,** *however much*; **om-endog, om-saa,** *although*, are used to denote a possible contingency; as
   selv om du har Retten paa din Side, bør du dog være forsigtig, *although you have right on your side you must be careful.*

Final.

Forat, *in order that.*
   hun satte Kaffe ud forat hun kunde faa lidt varmt om Morgenen, *she set out coffee in order that she might be able to get some hot in the morning.*

Saa at, *so that,* of consequence.

der var ganske stille saa at ikke et Blad rørte sig, *it was* (literally, *there was*) *so still that not a leaf moved.*

Uden at, *without.*

Røverne sagte til Gutten, at kunde han tage Oxen, uden at Manden fik vide om det, at saa at han ikke gjorde ham nogen Skade, saa skulde han være jævngod med dem, *the robbers said to the boy that if he could take the ox without the man's getting to know about it, and so that he did him no harm, why then, he should be on equal terms with them.*

Comparative.

Som, *as,* generally followed or preceded by **saa** in the principal sentence.

som man reder saa ligger man, *as you make your bed so you must lie in it.*
jeg skal gjøre det saa godt som jeg kan, *as well as I can.* Often omitted, as, saa godt jeg kan.

Ligesom, *just as.* **Alt som,** *quite as.* **Som om,** *as if.*

End, *than.*

Ingen har Fred længere end Ens Nabo vil, *no one has peace longer than his neighbour pleases.*
det gik anderledes end han havde tænkt, *it turned out differently from what he expected.*

Jo—jo, *by how much—by so much.*

jo før jo heller, *the sooner the better.*

Jo—desto, des, *by so much.*

jo før du taler med hende, desbedre, *the sooner you have a talk with her, the better.*
desmere man har desmere vil man have, *the more one has, the more one wants.*

INTERJECTIONS.

Besides the natural exclamations expressing pain, wonder, &c., as, **hei, hallo, au,** *Oh dear!* **aa, o, uf, oh, fy,** *for shame!* there are certain expletives, or complementary particles, expressing the more subtle shades of intention; such are

Jo, *yes.*

Du har jo været der? *you have been there, haven't you?*
der er han jo, *why, there he is.*
det er jo noget Snak, *that's nonsense, you know.*
han gik jo, han kunde jo ikke andet, *he went since he could not help it.*
der er ingen Tvivl om at han jo faar det, *there is no doubt but that he will get it.*
jo jo! *yes, I dare say.*
jo vist, *to be sure,* also ironical.
jo nok, *well, yes.* (See above, p. 91.)

Dog, *however.*

det er dog farligt, *it is dangerous though.*
luk dog den Dør, *do shut that door.*
du har dog faaet Brevet, *you have received the letter, I hope.*
Nei dog, *you don't say so!*
hvad er det dog? *what can it be?*
se dog, *only look!*
det er dog for galt, *it really is too bad.*
det skal jo dog engang gjøres, *it must be done sooner or later.*
hvor er hun dog ikke yndig, *how lovely she is, to be sure!*

Nok, *enough.*

vi har nok og mere end nok, *we have enough and more than enough.*
Nei, nu har jeg nok af det, *well, that beats all.*
du forstaar mig nok, *I am sure you understand me.*
du maa nok le ad det, *you may well laugh.*
jeg gad nok vide, *I should very much like to know.*
han finder nok Huset, *I dare say he will find the house.*
det kan nok gaa, *I dare say it will do.*

han kommer nok, *he will come, sure enough.*
det troer jeg nok, *I rather think so ; I believe you.*
ja nok, *well, why not ?*
det tænkte jeg nok, *I thought as much.*
sagte jeg det ikke nok? *didn't I tell you so ?*
om der var nok saa mange, *if there were ever so many.*
nok engang = engang til, *once more.*
nok engang saa stor, *as large again.*

Vel, *possibly, I suppose.*

han gjør det vel naar man beder ham derom, *I dare say he will do it when he is asked.*

du har ikke gjort det vel? *you haven't done it, have you?*

men Deres Hest spiser da vel ikke Østers gjør den vel? *but your horse surely doesn't eat oysters, does he ?*

Miscellaneous Particles and Exclamations.

vi kommer ikke tilbage før i Slutten af August. Ikke det? *we shall not come back before the end of August. Won't you really ?*
ikke for aldrig, *not for the world !*

om Forladelse, *I beg your pardon.*

ingen Aarsag, bryd Dem ikke om det, alt forladt, *All right! never mind, don't trouble yourself.*

det er et Vakkert Hus, ikke sandt ? *It's a fine house, isn't it ?*
det er en snil liden Pige, ikke sandt ? *She is a good little girl, isn't she ?*

Kapteinen var her igaar, *the captain was here yesterday.*
var han det ? *was he ?*

stakkars Barn ! *poor child !*
for en uskikkelig Gut ! *what a naughty boy !*
nu, hvordan likte du den ? *well ! how do you like it ?*
godt gjort, Gutten min ? *well done, my boy !*

III. SYNTAX.

The rules and principles of construction which are common to universal grammar need not be discussed here.

Only idiomatic constructions, and modes of expression that differ from English, or are otherwise noticeable, and such as have not been already illustrated, will be dwelt upon.

SYNTAX OF THE SIMPLE SENTENCE.

Concord.

The general rule is, that an **Adjective** used as a **predicate** agrees with the subject in gender and number ; as

>Huset er mit, *the house is mine.*
>Manden er gammel, *the man is old.*
>Barnet er uartigt, *the child is naughty.*
>Børnene ere uartige, *the children are naughty.*

That the **Verb** agrees with the subject in number; as

>Manden arbeider, *the man works.*
>Mændene arbeide, *the men work.*
>Træet voxer hurtig, *the tree grows fast.*
>Træerne voxe hurtig, *the trees grow fast.*

But in practice Concords are neglected in certain cases ; e. g. :—

The singular form of the Verb is constantly used with a plural subject; as **vi har**, instead of **vi have** ; **de er**, for **de ere**.

When I, *you*, or De, *you*, are used in speaking to a single person, the predicate is always in the singular number ; as

> I er ikke rigtig **klog**, Nabo, *you are not quite right in your head, neighbour.*

An Adjective in the superlative degree is not declined when it stands alone as a predicative word; as

> Dagene ere **længst** (not længste) om Sommeren, *the days are longest in summer.*

When a **Past Participle** stands adjectivally as a **predicate**, it agrees with the subject in number, and participles of the strong conjugation in gender also; as

> Bjørnungerne var **bundne** om Natten men gik **løse** om Dagen, *the bear cubs were tied up at night, but went loose in the daytime.*

In the same way the participle ought to agree with its subject in the compound tenses of the Verb, those namely, that are formed by the help of **være** and **blive**.

But the original relation of the participle to the subject is forgotten, and in the compound tenses the neuter of the participle is used without regard to the gender and number of the subject. This is the common usage in conversation, and is also frequently adopted in the written language; as

> Bjørnungerne blev **bundet** hver Aften, men **løst** igjen om Morgenen.

In tenses formed with the participle of **blive**, they write **blevet**, pronounced **bleet** and **blit**; e. g.

> Talen, Talerne, er blevet **skrevet**, *the speech, the speeches have been written.* They say also, Talerne er **blet skrevne**.

An **Adjective** standing as **predicate** of the **object**, as a rule agrees with the object in gender and number; e. g.

> de priste **ham lykkelig**, *they deemed him fortunate*; de priste **Barnet lykkeligt**; han priste **dem lykkelige**.

But in some cases the Adjective has become so closely united with the Verb that it is treated as a part of the Verb, and so is not declined; as

han har **mig kjær**, *he holds me dear.*
han har **os kjær**, *he holds us dear.*
man slap **Fangerne los**, *they released the prisoners.*

Personal Pronouns used as **predicates** are put in an oblique case; as

det er **mig**, *it is me.*   det er **os**, *it is us.*
er det **dig**? *is it you?*   det er **Eder**, *it is you.*
det var **ham, hende**, *it was him, her.*   det var **dem**, *it was them.*

Examples of Idiom in regard to Concord.

men det var dog alligevel ham, som havde slaaet Faderen fordærvet, ham var det, *but it was him, all the same, who had struck his (Arne's) father dead, yes 'twas him.*

den fremmede Skipper? Ja, hvor var han? Og kjendte han hende, eller var det blot hende, som kjendte ham? *then, the foreign captain? where was he? And did he know her, or was it only she that knew him?*

IMPERSONAL EXPRESSIONS.

An occurrence may be described without reference to a personal agent or patient by the passive alone; as

derom tvivles ikke, *of that (there) is no doubt.*

But generally **det**, *it*, or **der**, *there*, is used to supply the place of subject in the sentence; **det**, with Verbs in the active and passive voice; as

det er varmt, *it is hot.*   det dages, *day is breaking.*

der, with passives; as

der staar skrevet: du skal ikke slaa ihjel, *it is written thou shalt not kill.*

Der may be used when the subject is an appositive clause; as

der fortæller at han er død, *there (it) is rumoured that he is dead;*

but also **det**; as

    det fortaltes at han var død, *it was rumoured that he was dead.*

Det is sometimes used for **der**; as

    det kommer mere Regn, *it is more rain coming,* for, *there is.*

Der er is followed by a Pronoun in an oblique case; as

    der er dem som troer, *there are them that believe.*

In most cases the use of **det** and **der** in impersonal expressions corresponds with the use of *it* and *there* in English.

The following are exceptions:—

    Klokken er tre, *it is three o'clock.*
    Den er halv fem, *it is half-past four.*
    Den mangler ti minuter paa syv, *it wants ten minutes to seven.*
    Der er ti Miil herfra til Byen, *it is ten miles from here to the town.*
    Hvem er den unge Dame? det er min Søster, *who is that young lady? she is my sister.*
    Det er mine Børn, *they are (it is) my children.*
    Det var hans sidste Ord, *these were his last words.*

There are certain Verbs that are used both personally and impersonally; as

    jeg synes, *or,* det synes mig, *it seems to me.*
    jeg tykkes, det tykkes mig, *I am of opinion.*
    jeg undrer mig, jeg undres paa, det undrer mig, *I wonder, I am astonished at.*
    han harmedes, det harmede ham, *he was vexed.*
    jeg gyste, det gjøs i mig, *I shuddered.*
    feiler noget Dem? feiler De noget? *does anything ail you? do you ail anything?*

Among the impersonal expressions may be classed the constantly recurring use of the indefinite man, *one*; as

    naar man er træt holder man af at hvile, *when one is tired one likes to rest.*
    man kan ikke vide, *there's no knowing.*
    man maa ikke misforstaa mig, *let me not be misunderstood.*

Examples of Impersonal Expressions.

det er Dem som har røbet mig, *it is you who have betrayed me*.
der er ikke et Menneske at se, *there is not a creature to be seen*; but ikke et Menneske var at se, *there was not a man to be seen*.
der gives dem som tro, *there are those who think*.
herved er at mærke, *here (it) is to be remarked*.
hvis saa er, *if so be*.
om saa var, *if so (it) were*.
som sig hør og bør, *as is meet and proper*.
det er bedst jeg gaaer, *I had better go*.
der siges, *it is said*.
han vidste ikke hvad der var bedst, *he did not know what was best*.
han var Fisker, men dertil velstaaende Kjøbmand som havde Fartøi; det skulde være saadan en yndig, gammel Mand, ham var det nok værdt at staae i Tjeneste hos, *he was a fisherman, and a well-to-do merchant besides who had a ship; he was said to be such a nice old man, it would certainly be worth while to be in his service*.
jo, han skulde vide alt! For ham maatte ikke lyves! *yes, he should know all; before him there must be no lying!*
der hilses, og standses for hvert Skridt; Haandtryk vexles, og gode Budskab høres, *there is greeting and stopping at every step; handshakes are exchanged, and good tidings heard*.

THE SUBSTANTIVE.

Syntax of the Substantive in **apposition**.
The place of abode is added to the christian **name** and patronymic without a Preposition; as, **Lars Nilsen Ødegaard**.

The rank or profession is placed first; as
Foged Lie, *Sheriff Lie*; **Bisp Nikolaus,** *Bishop Nicolas*; **Presten Landstad** (with definite article), *the Priest Landstad*; **Konsul Kjeldsberg,** *Consul Kjeldsberg*.

Obs. In Old Norse the title is placed after the proper name; as **Haakon Jarl, Sverre Prest**; and the practice still remains in the vulgar language; as **Knut gjætergut,** *Knut, (the) shepherd*; **Jens Dreng,** *John, (the) serving man*. A very common vulgarism is the redundant use of **han** with a Noun; as **han Olaf, han Fader, hun Moder**.

Generally the name of a place used as a predicate is put in apposition, where we use the Preposition of; as **Øen Man,** *the Isle of Man*, **Kongeriget Norge,** *the kingdom of Norway*.

The **Genitive Case** in Norse, as in English, is sometimes expressed by the Preposition **af,** *of*, sometimes by the termination **s**.

But the inflected Genitive is more extensively used than in English; as

Englands Historie, *the history of England*.

The inflected form may be used in the Objective Genitive also; as

Døds Frygt, *the fear of death*.

Adjectives used substantively also take the inflected Genitive; as

den Fattiges Barn møder i den Riges aflagte Klader, og vises frem for at takke, *the poor (man's) child meets you in the rich one's cast-off clothes, and is exhibited by way of thanks*.

In some cases where in English we use the inflected Genitive, they prefer some other form of expression; as

vi gik ind til en Boghandler, *we went into a bookseller's.*
jeg traf hende hos din Broder, *I met her at your brother's.*

Sometimes the sign of the Genitive is omitted where we use it in English; as

et Par Handsker, *a pair of gloves*; et Stykke Brød, *a bit of bread.*

The form of the **Dative** and **Accusative** is the same where inflection appears, as in the case of personal pronouns; as **mig, dig, ham**, dat. or acc.

The Dative case, as in English, sometimes takes a Preposition, generally **til**, *to*, before it; sometimes it is used alone; e. g.

han gav sin Broder Bogen, *he gave his brother the book.*
han gav Bogen til sin Broder, *he gave the book to his brother.*

The Dative is often used without a Preposition, where in English a Preposition would be used; viz.

det er mig lige kjært, *it is all the same to me.*

Obs. In Old Norse there was an inflected form of the dative, still retained in some of the dialects of the peasantry; e. g.

han gav Bornom mat, *he gave the child food.*
han lærda Bornom at læsa, *he taught the child to read.*
Guten likjast Foreldrom, *the boy was like his parents.*
han hjælper Brodrom, *he helps his brother.*

The Accusative case, as in English, is used without a preposition in definitions of size, weight, and duration of time; as

Laxen veiede en Bismerpund, *the salmon weighed a Bismerpund*, i. e., *twelve pounds.*
han var borte fire Uger, *he was away four weeks;* also, han var borte i fire Uger.

But in certain expressions a preposition is inserted; as

Dampskibet gaar bare to Gange om Ugen, *the steamer goes only twice a week.*

I

Substantives used as above in defining measure do not take the plural inflection, except those ending in e singular; as **fire Tommer bred,** *four inches broad.*

Examples.

paa Afgrundens Rand, *on the brink of the abyss.*
Fædrelands Kjærlighed, *love of one's country.*
De maa agte paa andres Raad som veed bedre, *you must take heed of the advice of others who know better.*
en Ven af mig, *a friend of mine.*
en Fætter af os, *a cousin of ours.*
en Ven af min Fader, *a friend of my father's.*
et Glas Vand, *a glass of water.*
et Par Dage, *a couple of days.*
i Juli Maaned, *in the month of July.*
Raabet Brand, *the cry of fire.*
den første Mai, *the first of May.*
en lille Bitte Mand, *a little bit of a man.*
at sætte i Samfundets Ban, *to put out of the pale of society.*
Barnets Fader, or, Fader til Barnet, *the child's father,* or, *the father of the child.*
Kongens Søn, en Søn af Kongen, *the king's son, a son of the king.*
en Mørkets Gjerning, *a deed of darkness.*
Olaf den Helliges Død, *the death of Saint Olaf.*
for Ro og Freds Skyld, *for the sake of peace and quietness.*
en Sværm Bier, ogsaa en Sværm af Ansøgere, *a swarm of bees, also a swarm of suitors.*
en Pund Tobak, en Ladning Kul, *a pound of tobacco, a cargo of coal.*
en Masse Bøger, or, af Bøger, or, med Bøger, *a mass of books.*
ikke meget til Mand, *not much of a man.*
det var Karl til Mand, *that was a queer man.*
en Fant af en fordrukken Skomager, *a rascal of a drunken shoemaker.*
det havde været mig kjærere, *that would have been more pleasing to me.*
dette Liv blev mig en Byrde, *this life became a burden to me.*
han var mig som en Fader, *he was a father to me.*
jeg er Dem meget forbunden, *I am much obliged to you.*
jeg er mig selv nærmest, *I am nearest to myself.*

det hændte mig, *it happened to me.*
denne Bog tilhører mig, *this book belongs to me.*
det gaar ham godt, *it goes well with him.*
man gav sine Følelser Luft, *he gave vent to his feelings.*
som det en brav Mand egner og anstaar, *as is fitting and proper to a brave man.*
Frænde er Frænde værst, *kin to kin is most unkind.*
han gik tre Mil om Dagen, *he walked three miles in the day.*
Bogen koster en Krone, *the book costs a crown.*
han er ikke et Haar bedre end de Andre, *he is not a bit better than the others.*
han er kommen et godt Stykke paa Veien, *he has come a good piece of the way.*
han kom denne Vei, *he came this way.*

THE ARTICLE.

The use of the Articles, definite and indefinite, corresponds for the most part with the English use; but the following idioms must be noticed:

The **Indefinite Article** is omitted before a Noun substantive used as a predicate; as

    hun er Enke, *she is a widow.*
    hendes ældste Søn var Sagfører, *her eldest son was an attorney.*
    Arnes Fader blev Krøbling, *Arne's father became a cripple*;

and in certain other expressions where in English we should insert it; as

    en Kop uden Hank, *a cup without a handle.*
    med tungt Hjerte, *with a heavy heart.*
    at have Ret til, *to have a right to.*
    kjært Barn har mange Nævne, *a favourite child has many names.*
    maa jeg uleilige Dem med at give mig Fyrstykke? *may I trouble you for a light?*

The use of the **Definite Article** in Norse differs somewhat from its use in English, in the following cases.

The Definite Article is used in expressions of measure; as

    engang om Ugen, *once a week.*
    den koster ti Kroner Meteren *that costs ten crowns a yard.*
    hun har tusinde Kroner om Aaret, *she has 1000 crowns a year*;

also with Abstract Nouns; as

    Søvnen er Dødens Broder, *sleep is the brother of death.*
    Sommeren føder, Vinteren øder, *summer breeds, winter wastes.*
    Livet er kort, *life is short*;

with Nouns used in a general sense; as

    Klapper du Bonden napper han dig, *if you pat a peasant he will give you a nip.*
    Mennesket spaar, men Gud raar, *man proposes, God disposes*;

SYNTAX OF THE ARTICLE.

and where we use a Possessive Pronoun; as

> hun kastede sig i Armene paa mig, *she threw herself into my arms.*
> han gik med Hatten under Armen, *he went with his hat under his arm;*

in exclamations with a vocative; as

> her har Du Truget dit, Styggen! *here's your snow shoe, you ugly thing!*

Den, det, pl. de, is the form of the Definite Article always used before an Adjective; as

> den runde Jord, *the round world.*

den is used, and not the suffix en, with a substantive which is further defined by an infinitive, or by a relative; as

> jeg har ikke den Ære at kjende Dem, *I have not the honour of knowing you;*

with adjectives used substantively; as

> man skal ikke foragte de Smaa, *we must not despise the little ones;*

and with substantives simply, by the poets; as

> de Vover saa sagtelig trille, *the waves so gently murmur.*

But the definite **en** may be suffixed to a substantive following **al**, *all;* **hel**, *whole;* **selv**, *self;* **begge**, *both;* e. g.

> alt Folket, *or* det hele Folk; *all the people,* or, *the whole people.*
> hele Dagen, *or,* den hele Dag, *all the day.*
> selv Kongen, *the king himself.*
> han vil have Bugten og begge Enderne, *he will have his own way.*
> begge Brødrene, *both the brothers;*

and this use has been extended to substantives following other adjectives than the above; as

> midt inde i mørke tætte Skoven, *in the midst of the dark thick wood.*
> jeg seer ikke andet end Himmel og vilde Fjeldet, *I see only the sky and the wild field;*

sometimes **en** is suffixed after a Definite Article or Demonstrative Pronoun preceding; as,

> han vandt **det** ene Spillet efter det andet, *he won one game after another.*
> de gjorde ikke Veien lang, **de** Karlene, *they made no long journey of it, those fellows.*
> **denne** Jenten, *this lass.*

Den, det, is on the other hand sometimes omitted before Adjectives; as

> for tredie og sidste Gang, *for the third and last time.*
> med største Fornøielse, *with the greatest pleasure.*
> jeg havde ikke fjerneste Anelse derom, *I had not the most distant idea of it.*

THE ADJECTIVE.

The Adjective in Norse differs from the Adjective in English in the following points.

In Norse the Adjective distinguishes,
1. the neuter from the common gender,
2. the plural number from the singular,
3. the definite from the indefinite form,
4. the genitive case by inflection.

Syntactically, in Norse the Adjective, whether used as an attribute or as a predicate, agrees with its substantive in gender and number.

The Adjective, however, when used as a predicate, may follow the natural gender of the substantive; as

> da Pigebarnet var bleven saa stor, at hun kunde skjønne, *when the girl baby was grown big enough to take notice.*

But, as an attribute, it must always be in formal agreement with the substantive; as

> et stort Pigebarn, *a big girl baby.*

The Adjective is commonly in Norse, as in other languages, used with a substantive expressed; as

> en syg Mand, *a sick man.*

Idiomatically, it is sometimes used with the Pronoun **en**, *one*, in place of the substantive; as

> der boede en underlig graasprengt en paa den yderste nøgne Ø, *there dwelt a strange grizzled one (creature) on the outermost naked isle.*

This **en** is sometimes omitted; as

> der steg nogle Bobler op, endnu nogle, saa bare en stor, der brast, *there came up some bubbles, then some more, then one large one which burst.*

The Adjective itself may be used as a substantive and t͟ capable of being inflected in the genitive; as

>han kaldtes ' de Fattiges Fader,' *he was called the father of the*
>en Unge, *a young man.*
>den Rige, *the rich man.*
>den rige Styggen, *the rich ugly (fellow).*
>de syv Vise, *the seven wise men.*
>det Bedste er det Godes Fjende, *'tis better to let the well alone.*
>man skal ikke foragte de Smaa, *we must not despise the little.*
>de Unges Samfund, *the young men's society.*

THE PRONOUNS.

The following idioms are noticeable.

The **Possessive** Pronoun, **din**, *thine* (where we should use the Personal, *you*), is frequently joined to a vocative case, especially to express reproach or pity ; as

> Pedro gik lige under Træet, saa op, og raabte, 'kom ned med Dig, dit Skarn,' *come down with you, you wretch !*
> Du skulde kanske forstaae dit eget bedste, Du, **din** Nar ! *you must understand your own business best, you fool, you !*
> **Din** Tosse ! **din** Slusk ! **din** Hund ! *you booby ! you scamp ! you hound !*
> vil din Hund holde din Næse herfra ! *will you keep your nose off that, you dog !*

Min, *mine*, is used in the same way, to express pity ; as

> hvad skal det blive til mig, **min** arme Mand ? *what will become of me, poor me ?*
> Gud naade mig for dig, dit arme Pus ! *God have mercy on me for you, poor darling !*
> hvad skal jeg, **min** arme Mand, *or*, jeg arme Mand, gribe til ? *what shall I, poor wretch, have recourse to ?*

Obs. In many districts of Norway sin, sit, hans, hendes, are used instead of the genitive of the Substantive.

> Jephtha sin Datter, *Jephtha's daughter.*
> Gaarden hans Olaf, *Olaf his house.*

The **Personal Pronoun** of the third person is used for the second, in the colloquial form De, for du ; as

> hvad ønsker De min Herre ? *what do you want, sir ?*
> hvad ønske De, mine Herre ? *what do you want, gentlemen ?*

Dokke, Dokko (eder) are used in some districts of Norway in addressing superiors, instead of **De,** *you.*

Dere is also used as a Vocative ; as

> Oa ! kjære, goe, snille **Dere** ! jeg skal aldrig gjøre det mere, *Oh dear, good, kind, sir ! I will never do it again.*

Han, hun, is also frequently used for **Du,** in speaking to children, or dependants; as

ti stille, Jomfru Næsvis, jeg vil slet ikke høre paa **hendes Ræsonnement. Hun** er den impertinenteske Tøs i hele Institutet! *Hush! Miss Malapert! I will not listen to your excuses. You are the most impertinent hussy in the school!*

Relative. Som, *who, which,* is the Relative Pronoun most used.

Der, *who,* is used only as a subject; as

hun levede op som en **Plante der faar Vand,** *she revived like a plant that gets water.*

Hvem, when not interrogative, is used as objective only.

Hvo, hvad, followed by **som,** or **der,** become *whoso, whatever;* as

hvo som rører ved Beg, besmittes, *whoso meddles with pitch becomes defiled.*

Hvad like *what* in English, is sometimes interrogative; sometimes it combines in itself the antecedent and relative: as

hvad behager? *what do you please to want?*
jeg har gjort hvad jeg kunde, *I have done what I could.*

The Relative is often omitted, as in English (see p. 52, ante); as

hvem var det, Du talte med? *who was that you were talking to?*

Especially after a superlative; as

det Første han gjorde var, *the first thing he did was,* &c.

Sometimes even as the subject, where we insert the Relative; as

det er allerede det sjette Pund Kaffe, her er bleven fortæret i denne Barselstue, *that is already the seventh pound of coffee (that) there has been consumed in this room.*

The **Demonstrative** Pronoun is used for the relative, as we use *that,* for *which;* as

det jeg skrev, det skrev jeg, *that I have written, I have written.*

The **Reflexive** Pronoun **sig**, and the possessive **sin**, always refer to the subject in the third person; as

    han slog sig, *he struck himself.*
    de slog sig, *they struck themselves.*
    han tog sine Bøger, *he took his books.*
    de tog sine Bøger, *they took their books.*
    Mamma, Gutterne burde virkelig skamme sig, *mamma, the boys ought really to be ashamed of themselves.*
    vore Hatte ere her, lad os tage hver sin, *our hats are here, let us each take his own.*

When **De, Dem**, are used colloquially in the sense of *you*, then **Dem, Deres**, are used reflexively instead of sig, sin; as

    hvorledes, befinder De Dem? *how do you find yourself?*
    de har glemt Deres Stok, *you have forgotten your stick.*
    gaa Deres Vei! *go your way?*

Danish writers use **Deres** instead of **sin** even when the Pronoun refers to a subject in the third person plural; as

    de gik deres Vei, *they went their way.*
    de tog deres Bøger, *they took their (own) books.*
    de slog dem, *they beat themselves.*

THE VERB.

TENSES.

The **Historic Present**, as in other languages, is used in lively narrative, to describe past events.

The **Present** tense is constantly used **for the future**; as

han reiser imorgen, *he will start to-morrow.*
naar bliver De færdig? *when will you be ready?*
gaar du i Theatret iaften? *are you going to the theatre to-night?*
naar du modtager disse Linier, er jeg ikke mere her, *when you receive these lines I shall no longer be here.*

Skal *or* **vil** must however not be omitted where emphasis is required, or where an intention is attributed to the agent; as

Du skal gaa; jeg vil ikke gaa, *you shall go; I will not go.*

Skal, skulde, are used where in English we use *am to be, am going to, is said to be*; as

han skal gifte sig, *he is going to be married.*
Kongen skal være farlig syg, *the king is said to be dangerously ill.*
da han skulde til at dø, *when he was about to die.*
jeg skulde hænges men jeg fik Pardon, *I was to have been hanged but I obtained pardon.*

The **Perfect** Tense is used in Norse where we use the aorist of the indicative; as

hvem har opdaget America? *who discovered America?*

The **Past** tense is used instead of the present in certain cases, where it implies diffidence or courtesy on the part of the speaker; as

maatte jeg spørge, om han ikke har en Datter ved Navn Leonora? *might I ask* (for, *may I ask*) *whether he has a daughter called Leonora?*
det skulde jeg mene, *that's what I mean.*

And to express admiration; as

> nei, men det **var** underligte! *nay, but that is wonderful!*
> det **var saa** snilt du kom, *it is so good of you to have come,* or, *it was so good of you to come.*

Moods.

The **Indicative** mood is used for the **Subjunctive** in oblique oration after a principal Verb in the past tense; as

> han lovede at komme naar jeg gav (for skulde give) det aftalte Tegn, *he promised to come when I gave (for should give) the appointed sign.*

And this usage is extended to the corresponding tenses when pluperfect, as

> han lovede at komme naar han **havde** spist, *he promised to come when he had eaten his meal* (i. e. *should have eaten*).

Skulde *or* **vilde** as the sign of the imperfect subjunctive, is generally retained in the apodosis, but may be omitted in both protasis and apodosis; as

> han sagde, at hvis han fik udført sine Forretninger idag, saa **vilde** han allerede imorgen reise tilbage, *he said that if he managed to get his business finished to-day, he would return home to-morrow,* or, saa **reiste** han allerede imorgen tilbage.

Instead of **skal, vil have**; **skulde, vilde have**, the auxiliary **faar** *or* **fik** may be used; as

> naar jeg faar spist skal jeg komme, *when I have done my meal I will come.*
> han sagde at han skulde komme bare han fik spist, *he said he would come as soon as he had finished his meal.*

The **Optative** mood is used mostly in formal expression of a wish, in prayers, blessings, and the opposite; as

> Kongen leve! *long live the king!*
> evig du stande, Elskte blandt Lande! *mayst thou last for ever, dearest of lands!*

In colloquial language **gid**, is generally used; as

> gid Fanden havde ham! *the deuce take him!*

This mood is also used in concessions; as

> man sige hvad man vil, *people may say what they like.*

Infinitive. At, *to*, the sign of the infinitive, is omitted after the auxiliaries **skal, vil, maa, kan, tør,** as in English. It is also omitted after **burde,** *ought*; **lade,** *to cause*; **monne,** *to avail*; **gider,** *want to*; as jeg gad vide, *I should like to know*; after **faar** meaning *must*; as det faar gaa som det kan, *that must go as it best can*; and in the Norwegian idiom, also after **pleier,** *I am wont*; and **orker,** *I am capable of.*

The auxiliary infinitive **have** may be omitted altogether in the compound pluperfect subjunctive, after **kunde, skulde, vilde, burde, gad**; as

> jeg skulde sagt, *I should (have) said*; *for*, have sagt.
> hun kunde hørt en Naal falde, *she could (have) heard a pin fall.*
> jeg gad vist, *I should like to (have) known.*

But it is correct to retain it; as

> skulde det have været Katten? *could it have been the cat?*

A Verb of motion in the infinitive may be omitted after **maatte, skulle, ville**; as

> han maatte afsted, *he was obliged to leave.*

The infinitive with **at,** *to*, is used as a Noun, as in other languages.

Especially it is used where in English we use the verbal substantive, or gerund, ending in **ing**; as

> det kalder jeg at slaa to Fluer med eet Smæk, *I call that killing two birds with one stone.*
> jeg kunde ikke lade være at smile, *I could not help smiling.*
> jeg er færdig med at tale, *I have done speaking.*

Post efter Post kommer uden at bringe noget Svar, *post after post comes without bringing any answer.*
dette er langt fra at være sandt, *this is far from being true.*
jeg bad ham give mig Bogen istedenfor at læse paa sig, *I bad him give me the book instead of reading it to himself.*
ved nærmere at overveie Sagen er jeg kommen til en anden Mening, *on considering the case more closely I have come to a different conclusion.*

Sometimes an exegetical sentence instead of the infinitive is introduced by **at**, *that*, where we use the verbal substantive in **ing**; as

der gik ikke en Dag uden at jeg besøgte ham, *not a day passed without my visiting him.*
at den fremmede traadte ind i Værelset overraskede mig meget, *the stranger's entrance quite took me by surprise.*
jeg havde ikke hørt noget om at han var kommen, *I had not heard anything about his coming,* or, *having come.*

Participles. The *Present* Participle is not used, as it is in English, with an auxiliary to form the continuous or non-aorist tense, but either the simple form of the Verb, or a circumlocution is used; as

hvad bestiller du her? *what are you doing here?*
Vinden blæste friskt ifra Land, *the wind was blowing fresh from the land.*
Dørene holdt paa at falde af Hængslerne, *the doors were falling from their hinges.*
Huset holder paa at bygges, *the house is building.*

But the Present Participles of **ligge, staae, sidde, gaae**, are used with **bliver** to express a continuous action or state; as

hun blev siddende, *she remained sitting.*

If however another Verb is added to the predication, it is put in the infinitive mood, instead of the indicative; as

hun blev siddende og **sye**, *she went on sitting and sewing* (lit. *to sew.*)

The absolute use of the *Passive* participle (ablative absolute) is rare in Norse, being chiefly confined to **sagt, talt**, and the like.

>rent udsagt, han holder mig for en Nar, *said out (to speak out) clearly, he takes me for a fool.*
>alt vel overveiet, bliver dit Forslag det bedste, *all considered, your proposal is the best.*

Undtagen, *except*, originally a participle absolute, has become a Preposition.

Voice.

The **Active** voice is used where we use the passive, after **lade**; as

>han lod et stort Skib bygge, *he had a large ship*, or, *caused a large ship to be built.*

Also after **er, var**, implying *ability, fitness* and the like; as

>der var ingen at se, *there was no one to be seen.*
>han er ikke at spøge med, *he is not to be trifled with.*
>dette er ikke til at le ad, *this is not to be laughed at.*
>det var at vente, *that was to be expected.*
>gjort Gjerning staar ikke til at ændre, *a deed done cannot be mended.*

The **Passive**, in the inflected form, has sometimes a reflexive or reciprocal meaning; as

>han kjededes ved Livet, *he was tired of life.*
>nøies med det I have, *be content with such things as ye have.*
>naar Krybben er tom, bides Hestene, *when the manger is empty the horses bite each other.*
>vi sees igjen, *we shall see each other again.*

Some Verbs, chiefly those of the first class of strong verbs, avoid the inflected form in the past indicative passive; as

>der blev drukket, *there was drinking*; *never*, der drakkes.
>en Vise blev sunget, *there was a song sung*; *never*, der sanges.
>han blev hjulpen, *he had help given him*; *never*, han hjalpes.

SYNTAX OF THE VERB.

The form in es of the passive is mostly used as an aorist, not as a continuous tense; as

> Poeter fødes, siger man, *poets are born, they say.*
> en Ven kjendes i Nød, og ei i Springdands, *a friend is known in time of need, not at a country dance;* or, *merrymaking.*
> der skrives nu mange Komedier, *there are many plays written nowadays.*

In some Verbs however the form in **es** implies a state; as

> at blues, *to be bashful.* ræddes, *to be afraid.* færdes, *to be on a journey.* fattes, *to be wanting.* synes, *to seem.*

The form in **es** of the infinitive passive is used with auxiliaries, as, **skal, vil, kan,** in aorist sense; as

> han gjorde hvad gjøres kunde, *he did whatever could be done.*
> Liv for Liv maa bødes, *a life must be paid for a life.*
> denne Ordning kan med Lethed forandres, *this arrangement can easily be altered.*

The compound form, with **bliver, er,** is used mostly of a definite action or state; as

> denne Ordning kan let blive forandret, *this arrangement can easily be altered* (implying an intention to alter it).
> jeg beder om at det maa blive gjort strax, *I beg that this may be done directly.*
> Gutten blev kaldt Ole efter sin Fader, *the boy was called Ole after his father.*

But,

> i Klostret kaldtes han Broder Martin, *in the monastery he was called Brother Martin.*

SYNTAX OF THE COMPOUND SENTENCE.

The use and meaning of the Conjunctions and other particles that connect sentences, coordinate and subordinate, have been explained above.

The logical moods, or forms of thought, upon which Syntax is based, are not peculiar to Norse, or to any one language, and therefore need not be discussed here.

The following points deserve attention, mostly as differing from the English idiom.

When the **principal sentence** is a **negative** one, the dependent explanatory sentence beginning with at, *that*, assumes a negative character by taking jo; as

    jeg nægter ikke at jeg jo har en honnet Ambition, *I do not deny that I have an honest ambition.*

    der er ingen Tvivl om at han jo faar det, *there is no doubt but that he will get it.* (See pp. 91, 105.)

Explanatory sentences both modal and infinitive, **beginning with at**, are much used in Norse, where in English we use some other construction, generally a verbal substantive in **ing**; as

    hvor du er god at du besøger mig! *how good you are to come and see me!*

    jeg er daarlig at jeg staar her og taler med Jer, *I am a fool to stand here and talk with you.*

    der gaar ingen Dag, at jeg jo fortryder over ti Gange, at jeg har taget hende i Kost, *not a day passes without my repenting ten times over of having taken her as a lodger.*

    der er ingen Regel uden at den har sine Undtagelser, *or,* der er ingen Regel som jo har sine Undtagelser, *there is no rule without its exceptions.*

At may be omitted, usually where *that* would be omitted in corresponding English; as

    hvad mener du jeg tænker paa? *what do you suppose I am thinking about?*

SYNTAX OF THE COMPOUND SENTENCE. 131

SUBORDINATE SENTENCES.

TEMPORAL.

For Temporal Conjunctions see above p. 101 and for Adverbs p. 89.

Sometimes a Preposition is used as if it were a Conjunction; as

> **fra** jeg var et Barn, har jeg kunnet glæde mig ved at see Folk trækkes i Arrest, *from the time when I was a child, I have always been able to derive pleasure from seeing people taken up.*

Da is the word generally used to express *when*, as a relative; as

> der var en Tid da han pleiede at besøge mig, *there was a time when he used to visit me.*

Som or **at** may be substituted for **da**, or the relative may be omitted altogether; as

> nu du siger det saa husker jeg det, *now you mention it, I remember it.*

CAUSAL.

Besides the ordinary forms of expressing cause, by **fordi, da, siden,** &c. (see p. 102), we meet with the following.

> saa træt som jeg nu er kan jeg intet gjøre, *tired as I am now I can do nothing.*
>
> ' Ve dig saa sort du er,' sagde Gryden til Lerpotten, '*bad luck to you because you are so black,' said the gridiron to the earthen pot.*

Fordi properly signifies an actual material cause; as

> det er vaadt fordi det har regnet, *it is wet, because it has rained.*

Da, and the other particles denote rather an inferred cause; as

> da det er vaadt maa det have regnet, *since, seeing that it is wet, it must have rained.*

K 2

Naar, *when,* may be used like **siden,** *since,* as a causal conjunction; as

> jeg maa vel tro det, naar du siger mig det, *I must believe it, of course, since you say so.*

Conditional.

The protasis is generally introduced by one of the following Conjunctions, **dersom, hvis, saafremt, ifald, forsaavidt, naar, om,** *if,* or by **hvis ikke, medmindre, uden,** *if not, unless,* and the apodosis by **saa,** or, **da,** *then, in that case* ; as

> hvis en Hund gjøer een Gang udi Tide, saa bjæffer og skjæder den hundrede Gange udi Utide, *if a dog barks once at the right time, it yaps and yelps a hundred times at the wrong.*
>
> om jeg mindes ret saa har jeg seet dit Ansigt før, *if I remember right I have seen your face before.*

Notice, that in these cases the nominative follows the Verb in the apodosis, because the apodosis comes last, and precedes the Verb in the protasis whenever a Conjunction is used.

But very often the Conjunction, signifying *if,* is omitted. The hypothesis then takes the form of a question, and has the Verb before its subject; as

> var min Søn hjemme vilde han ikke taale dette, *if my son were at home he would not put up with this.*

The same mode of expressing a condition, without the Conjunction, is sometimes used in English; as, *should the books arrive to-morrow, you will be able to send them off on Wednesday.* But the form is much more common in Norse.

> nu drikker du din Thee, maaskee faaer du et Eventyr, *now if you will drink your tea, perhaps I will tell you a story.*
>
> Lærer hun formeget for sin Stand, har hun dermed naaet en anden Stand, *if she gets too much learning for her own rank in life, she is thereby brought nearer to another rank.*
>
> han gløttede ind gjennem Glasgluggen i Døren, hver Gang han drev

SUBORDINATE SENTENCES. 133

forbi, og var der saa kommen en Kunde, afsluttede han Spillet, og gik ind, *he peeped in through the pane of glass in the door, every time he went by, and if there was a customer there, he stopped (or, used to stop) playing, and went in.*

The indicative imperfect and pluperfect are often used in the apodosis of a conditional sentence, when we should expect the subjunctive ; as

dersom jeg kunde, saa gjorde jeg det, *if I could I would do it*; for vilde gjøre.
dersom jeg bare turde, gik jeg straks, *if I only dared I would go directly.*
dersom jeg havde vidst dette, var jeg reist strax, *if I had known this I would have gone away directly.*
hvis Eieren havde været tilstede kunde han gjort det selv, *if the owner had been present he could have done it himself*; for kunde han have gjort. (See also pp. 138, 125.)

Examples of Conditional Construction.

havde ikke et Par gamle Husmandsfolk, som han havde været god imod, nu taget sig af ham, saa var han bleven liggende uden Hjælp, *had not an aged cottager and his wife, to whom he had shown kindness now taken charge of him, he would have been lying there without help.*
var det ikke fordi Moderen sad inde, havde han maatte græde af Utaalmod, *had it not been for the fact that his mother sat in the room, he must have wept with impatience.*
det samme syntes gamle Knud, da han fik høre derom, og han mente tillige, at var der ingen anden, som kunde binde ham, saa skulde han og hans Sønner forsøge, *the same thought old Knut, when he came to hear of it, and he resolved moreover, that if there was no one else who could bind the fellow fast, he and his sons would have a try.*
rode han ud og forbi Tangen der borte, lagde saa til paa den andre siden af Fjældet, var der altid Raad til at komme op, skjønt der rigtignok var saa brat, at Geden gik der med Nød, og hun pleier dog ikke at være undselig til Fjælds, (*he thought that) if he were to row out and pass the spit of land yonder, and then made for the other side of the fell, there was always some means of getting up,*

although it was so steep, it is true, that a goat could hardly clamber that way, and a goat, you know, is not wont to be very shy about fell climbing.

Concessive.

Concessive clauses are introduced by the following Conjunctions, **skjønt, endskjønt, omendskjønt, uagtet, hvorvel,** *albeit,* **fast,** *although,* **endda,** *even still,* **om, om selv, om end, om endog, om saa, end** (in combination with a relative) **saa,** *ever, yet.*

Herren er kjendt af alle, skjøndt Herren kjender faa, *the gentleman is known to all, though the gentleman knows but few.*

jeg vilde mari ikke være i Hans sted, om man gav mig to Mark, *I would not in truth be in Hans' place, if any one would give me two marks.*

hvor du end er saa vogt du at være drukken, *wherever you are take care you don't get drunk.*

vi sees, om ikke før, saa til næste Aar, *we shall see each other next year, if not before.*

er han lam, er han stam, har han Penge, gaar han fram, i. e. om han end er lam, gaar han dog frem, hvis han har Penge, *although he is lame, although he stammers, yet he gets along well enough if he has money. 'Tis money makes the mare to go.*

To denote an actual concession, they use **skjøndt, uagtet, hvorvel, fast, endda;** as

Krudtet vilde ikke fænge, fast det gnistrede af Flinten og Stjaalet, *the powder refused to ignite, although sparks were struck from the flint and steel.*

jeg har kjendt et Par Ægtefolk, som levede yderst lykkelig med hinanden, uagtet Manden var stokdøv, *I knew a married couple who lived very happily together, although the man was as deaf as a post.*

To denote a **contingency or possible condition,** they use **om, selv om, om end, om endog, om saa,** *even if,* and **saa** (with relative) **end,** *however much;* as

SUBORDINATE SENTENCES.

selv om du har Retten paa din Side, bør du dog være forsigtig, *even if you have right on your side you ought still to be careful.*
Guld er Guld, hvor det end findes, og Lærdom er Lærdom af hvis Mund den end flyder, *gold is gold wherever it is found, and wisdom is wisdom from whose mouth soever it flows.*

Saa may be used without **som** to follow—*however, for all*; as

han maatte gjøre det saa nødig han vilde, *he was obliged to do it however reluctantly (little as he wished it).*
saa ulærd jeg er, saa veed jeg dog at Amsterdam ligger i Holland, *unlearned as I am I know that Amsterdam is in Holland.*

The subjunctive mood may be used alone in a concessive sense; as

man sige hvad man sige vil, det var dog godt gjort, i. e. hvad man end siger, *people may say what they like, but it was well done.*

Where there are several alternatives, for each of which the principal sentence stands equally good, they use **hvad enten, eller**; as

hvad enten det skal briste eller bære, saa maa det nu ske, *whether it will break or bear, it must be done now.*
enten jeg er glad eller bedrøvet, vred eller blid saa kan man altid læse det af min Ansigt, *whether I am glad or sorry, angry or calm, you can always read it in my face.*

FINAL.

Sentences denoting purpose or intention are introduced by the Conjunction '**forat**' (in the older language **paa det at**) either with infinitive mood, *in order to*, or with subjunctive clause, *in order that*; as

for ikke at glide tog vi vore Sko af, *in order not to slip we took our shoes off.*
for at enhver Misforstaaelse kan forebygges vil jeg endnu tilføie et Ord, *in order that all mistakes may be prevented, I will add one word.*

Consequent.

Sentences that denote a consequence are introduced by **saa at,** *so that.*

Saa is commonly disjoined from **at**; and at is frequently omitted; as

> Fjeldet skyggede saa at Solen ikke kunde skinne ind, *the fell was clouded over so that the sunshine could not penetrate.*
> Manden blev saa ræd at han rullede overende, *the man was so frightened that he tumbled head over heels.*
> der faldt noget ned i Maden saa han mistede Madlysten, *something fell into the dish, so that he lost his appetite for the meat.*

Sometimes the sequence is expressed by the infinitive, after **saa at,** *so as to*; as

> vær saa venlig at vise os paa ret Vei, *be so good as to show us the right way.*

or by a coordinate sentence; as

> vær saa venlig og vis os paa ret Vei, *be so good and show us the right way.*

In a clause consequent on a principal sentence containing a negative, **at jo,** is sometimes used for **at ikke**; as

> Intet er saa galt at det jo er godt for noget, *nothing is so bad that it is not good for something.*
> Blodet er aldrig saa tyndt, det er jo tykkere end Vand, *i. e.,* at det ikke er, *blood is never so thin that it is not thicker than water.* (See p. 130.)

Comparative.

Sentences implying a comparison are connected by **som, ligesom, end,** or **jo, som** being usually preceded by **saa** in the principal sentence; as

> det forholder sig saa som jeg siger, *it is as I say.*

SUBORDINATE SENTENCES.

> han er saa god som Dagen er lang, *he is as good as the day is long.*
> jeg skal gjøre det saa godt jeg kan, *I will do it as well as I can.*

Som om is used where the comparison is with an imaginary case; as

> han bar sig ad som om han var gal, *he behaved himself as if he were mad.*

the **om** is sometimes omitted; as

> han lod som han sov, *he pretended to be asleep.*

End, *than*, is used after comparatives, after **andet**, *other*, and the like; as

> Ingen har Fred længere end Ens Nabo vil, *no one has peace longer than his neighbour likes.*
> det gik anderledes end vi tænkte, *that turned out differently from what we expected.*
> faa Mennesker vil være andet end taknemmelige derfor, *few people will be other than grateful for it.*

Likeness of proportion is denoted by a comparative with **desto**, or **jo**, in the principal sentence, and a comparative with **jo** in the subordinate; as

> jo argere Skalk jo bedre Lykke, *the greater the rogue, the better the luck.*
> jo mere man har desmere man vel have, *the more a man has the more he wants.*
> jo før jo heller, *the sooner the better.*

Efter hvert som, *in proportion as*, is used in the same signification; as

> det gik bedre efter hvert som han fik mere Øvelse, *it went better as he got more practice.*

ELLIPSE.

The following are the commonest forms of ellipse in Danish and Norwegian.

Most of them have been already noticed in reference to the constructions in which they severally occur.

Verb of motion omitted; as

hvor skal De hen? *where are you going?*
jeg skal strax tilsengs, *I shall go to bed directly.*
da slap Signe—Petra ud, men Signe efter. Begge ind paa Signes Kammer, *then Signe let go—Petra (rushed) out, but Signe (followed) her. Both (ran) into Signe's room.*

Also with imperative, as in English; as

af sted med dig! *off with you!*
op Smed, ind med dig strax! *up Smith, in with you quick!*

Inceptive Verb omitted. This usage is a kind of historic infinitive.

bedst som det var fik Kjærringen væltet Tjæregryden over den Underjordiske. Hun til at huje og skrige, *just in the middle of it all the old crone managed to upset the tar-pot over the elf. She began to howl and screech.*

Sometimes the governing Verb, such as **lagde, satte, tog**, is inserted in one clause and omitted in the other; as

i det Samme satte Veslefrik til at stryge paa Felen, og Lensmanden til at dandse, *at the same time Veslefrik set to work to scrape his fiddle, and the lensman (began) to dance.*
Dagen efter sluttede Arne sin Arbeide, og reise hjem, *next day Arne finished his work and (proceeded) to go home.*
Hans var da færdig og blev siddende og se, *Hans had finished, and remained sitting and looking,* (*for*, holdt paa at se).

Auxiliary Verb omitted.

dersom jeg kunde, saa gjorde jeg det, *if I could do it, I would* (*for*, vilde gjøre det).

ELLIPSE.

men der var ingen Vei at gaae for Pigerne, de vilde faaet Klæderne revne itu, *but there was no path there for the girls to walk on, they would (have) got their clothes torn (for,* vilde have faaet).

Du kunde gjort det selv, *you could have (done) it yourself (for,* have gjort).

jeg gad vidst, *I should like (to have) known.*

han bad sig fritaget, *he begged to be excused.*

det havde været *(for,* skulde have været) mig kjærere, *that would have been more agreeable to me.*

The Verb is omitted in the phrase **ikke det?** *isn't it? don't you? haven't you?*

Substantive omitted, with Adjective, or participle; as

den fattige, *the poor man.*
de Smaa, *the little children.*
den Vises Sten, *the philosopher's stone.*
en Reisende, *a traveller.*
den fattiges Sørger og Glæder, *the poor man's sorrows and joys.*
Gamlen, *the old man,* Blakken, Brunen (of horses, as in English), *the brown, the bay, the grey;*

to avoid repetition, where in English we should use **one**.

The sign of the person [*my, your, her, him, them*] is omitted and **selv** is used alone as an Adjective; as

jeg skal selv samme Vei, *I am going the same way myself.*
Kapteinen selv har fortalt meg det, *the captain himself told me.*

Preposition omitted.

en Flaske Øl, *a bottle of beer.*
han er' flere Sprog mægtig, *he is master of many languages.*

Conjunction omitted. In the protasis of a conditional sentence, the sign of hypothesis, as **hvis, dersom**, is very often left out.

han var kommen før, havde han før været hjemme, *he would have come before (if) he had been at home before.*

The second conjunction **som**, *as*, in a comparative clause is sometimes omitted; as

jeg skal gjøre det saa godt jeg kan, *I will do it as well (as) I can.*

Also **da, som, der,** *when, as,* temporal; as

> en Høst de reiste hjem fra Sæteren klædte han sig i fuld Mundering, *one autumn (when) they came home from the sæter he dressed himself in full uniform.*

Also, **at,** *that,* after **saa.**

> jeg skal ringe for hans Øren saa han skal høre det, *I will make such a ringing in his ears (that) he shall hear it.*

The Details of the Syntax, in a comparative sentence, may be omitted where no ambiguity would arise; as

> Pedersens Ko spiser Sildehoveder som en Sælhund (spiser dem), og man kan give den Tang som Græs, *Pedersen's cow eats herringheads, like a seal, and you can feed her on seaweed like grass.*

The Article is omitted after the Pronoun **hvilken,** expressing admiration; as

> hvilken smuk Dag! *what a fine day!*

PLEONASM.

The Definite Article is sometimes used redundantly, being suffixed to a Substantive which is preceded by an Adjective in the definite form; as

> de som var i den storste Baaden, *those who were in the largest boat.*

Also to the **Substantive** used exegetically in the definite form; as

> han var altid haard til at lede efter Skatte **den Karlen**! *he was always keen at seeking after treasure (was) that fellow.*

The Pronoun, han or **hun**, is sometimes redundant, being prefixed to a Noun; as

> han Olaf, *he Olaf.* han Fader, *he father.* hun Mor, *she mother.*
> der kan du faa **hende** Synnøve at se, sagde Faderen, *there you can see Synnöve, said his Father.*

also, **sig**; as

> hvad forstaar Bønder **sig** paa Agurk? *that is caviar to the general.*

The Preposition til is inserted before the sign of the infinitive, as *for to* is used in English.

> han har mykje **te aa** (for til at gjøre), gjere, *he has muckle for to do.*
> han staar ikke **til** at redde, *he does not admit of being rescued.*

Also the **Infinitive** is used as an expletive; as

> han veed meget af en Bonde **at være**, *he is well informed for a peasant.*

ORDER.

The order of words and clauses in Norse is on the whole the same as in English; that is to say, it is the natural order, as distinguished from the periodical style of Latin.

Some writers however affect the German method of combining a variety of clauses in one long sentence; e.g.

> Allerede et Par Mil ovenfor Assibagti begyndte Furutræer at blande sig med Birkeskoven, mellem hvilke de blive hyppigere og hyppigere, indtil de, en halv Milsvei ovenfor det nævnte Sted, paa Elvens nordlige Side, gaa over i mere-sammenhængede-men-dog-altid med-Birkeskov-mere-eller-mindre-blandede Furuskovbestande, der optage de-alt-højere og-højere-blivende Lier og Aasskraaninger lige til henimod Elvens Udløb i Tana.
>
> *A couple of miles further up than Assibakti scattered pine-trees begin to mingle with the birch-wood, in which they gradually become more frequent, until, about half a mile above that place, on the northern side of the river, they merge into more continuous but still always with birch-mingled pine-forest, which occupies the ever higher and higher lying slopes and ridges as far as the outlet of the river into the Tana.*

But the order of words differs from the English in the following cases :—

Position of the Object.

When the Predicate is made up of the Verb **være**, *to be*, and an Adjective, or other predicative word, the **Object** is put **between** them; as

> hun er **mig** kjær, *she is dear to me.*
> han var **alle** en Gaade, *he was a riddle to all.*
> de vare **ham** paa Spor, *they were on his track.*

In clauses beginning with **hvo, hvad,** *whatsoever, whatever,* the **Object** may be put **before** the Verb; as

> hvo lidet har lidet faar, *who little has little gets.*

ORDER.

A **Negative** word used in the Predicate is always placed between the auxiliary and the verb; as
>jeg har **ingen** seet, *I have seen nobody.*
>jeg kan **intet** gjøre, *I can do nothing.*

Position of the Subject.

In exclamations the Subject is sometimes put **between** the Adverb and the Predicate which the Adverb qualifies; as
>hvor **du** er snild! *how kind you are!*

The **Nominative Case** is put **after** the Verb when some word or expression other than the subject begins the sentence; as
>den Mand **kjender jeg** ikke, *I do not know that man.*
>paa den anden Dag **ledte hun** efter sin Søn, *the next day she went to look for her son.*
>derpaa **var alt** stilt, *then all was still.*
>sit Navn **skrev han** ikke længer Olsen, men Ohlsen, *he no longer wrote his name Olsen but Ohlsen.*
>nu **seer du** Kirken, *now you see the church.*

Accordingly the **Nominative** is put **after** the Verb in the principal sentence, if the subordinate sentence comes first; as
>naar han om Kvælden kom hjem, **var Faderen** ofte fuld, *when he came home of an evening, his father was frequently drunk.*
>da han havde betalt Regningen, **reiste han**, *when he had paid the bill, he went away.*

So the **Nominative** comes **after** the Verb in apodosis, if the protasis comes first; as
>hvis han havde fulgt mit Raad **havde han** nu været en holden Mand, *if he had followed my advice he would now have been a well-to-do man.*

But
>**han var** ikke bleven rød hvis hun havde været ham ligegyldig, *he would not have blushed if she had been equally to blame with him.*

The **Nominative** comes **after** its Verb in protasis when the conjunction, **hvis, dersom,** *if,* is omitted; as

> **har du** Lyst, saa kan du nok faae Tjeneste hos os, *if you like you can take service here.*
> han var kommen før, **havde han** før været hjemme, *he would have come before, had he been at home.*

Position of Adverb.

The Adverb comes **after** the Verb or its auxiliary in principal sentences; and comes **before** the Verb or its auxiliary in dependent sentences; as

> Ulykken **kommer sjelden** alene, *misfortunes seldom come alone.*
> hun **vovede næppe** at tale, *she hardly dared to speak.*
> han sagde at han **aldrig kunde** glemme hende, *he said that he could never forget her.*

Position of the Negative.

In certain cases the order of the Norse has, *not can, not could, not will, not shall, not would,* &c., where in English we say, *can not, could not, will not.*

The **Negative** comes **before** the Verb or its auxiliary if it has one,

In dependent sentences,
In oblique narrative,
In protasis where the conjunction is expressed.

Examples of **Negative before** the Verb.

> jeg er bange for at jeg **ikke kan** komme, *I am afraid that I cannot come.*
> den kan ogsaa tygge som **ikke har** alle Tænder, *a man may manage to chew who has not all his teeth.*
> Peder sagde at han **ikke kunde** bede om Forladelse, da han **ikke havde** gjort noget galt, *Peter said that he could not beg pardon, since he had not done anything wrong.*

Nils vil ikke gaa til ham hvis han **ikke bliver** bedt til at komme, *Nils will not go to him if he is not asked to go.*

jeg skulde have kommet før hvis jeg **ikke havde** været borte fra Byen, *I should have come before, if I had not been absent from town.*

hun havde sagt at Datteren **ikke kunde** komme, *she had said that her daughter could not come.*

hvis I **ikke skynder** Eder, kommer I forseent, *if you don't make haste you will be too late.*

vi kunde være blevet dræbte hvis vi **ikke var** komne forseent til Toget, *we might have been killed if we had not arrived too late for the train.*

han siger at han **ikke kan** tilgive ham, *he says that he cannot forgive him.*

nu, jeg haaber I **ikke er** bange for at sige Sandheden, *now I hope you are not afraid to tell the truth.*

naar den Mand **ikke kan** hjælpe ham, saa kan ingen, *if that man can't help him, no one can.*

idag sagde han at han **ikke havde** noget Haab om at redde ham, *today he said that he had no hope of saving his life.*

han siger han **ikke kan** gjøre noget. Jeg er sikker paa at han **ikke kunde** gjøre mere end de andre, *he says he cannot do anything. I am sure that he could not do more than the others.*

jeg sagde Dem mange Gange at De **ikke burde** bo i den Gade, *I told you many times that you ought not to live in that street.*

The **Negative** comes **after** the Verb or its auxiliary if it s one

In principal sentences,
In oratio recta,
In apodosis of conditional sentences.

Examples of **Negative after** the Verb.

jeg lagde **ikke** Mærke til at Præsten var tilstede, *I did not observe that the priest was present.*

jeg har **ikke** hørt nogen banke paa, *I have not heard anyone knock.*

naar De flytter til den borteste Ende af Byen **kan** De **ikke** vente at see Folk hver Dag, *if you go to live at the furthest end of the town, you cannot expect to see folks every day.*

L

nei, jeg **mener ikke** det, *no, I don't mean that.*

men da han saa at Værelset var fuldt af Folk, **kunde han ikke** tænke paa at komme nær Kaminen, *but seeing the room was full of people, he could not see any chance of getting near the fireplace.*

han **havde ikke** siddet der læng før Staldkarlen kom ind igjen og raabte at Hesten **ikke havde** rort Østerne, *he had not sat there long before the ostler came in again, and cried out that the horse had not touched the oysters.* But,

kanske den **ikke var** sulten, sagde Herren, *perhaps (it may be that) he was not hungry, said the gentleman.*

jeg **kunde ikke** gjøre andet, sagde han, skjøndt jeg vidste du **ikke vilde** like det, *I could not do anything else, said he, although I knew you would not like it.*

The **Negative** comes **after** the Verb or its auxiliary; also In questions, as in English.

In protases where the conjunction is suppressed, which are in the form of a question; as

kommer han ikke med? *isn't he coming with us?*
kommer han ikke med saa **faar han ikke** Aftensmad, *if he does not come with us he wont get any supper.*

Position of the Article.

The Definite Article *the* is suffixed to Substantives, as Katt**en**, *the cat*; Katt**ene**, *the cats*; Barn**et**, *the child*.

The Definite Article is placed before Adjectives, as **den** store Hund, *the big dog*.

The Indefinite Article precedes both Substantives and Adjectives, as in English.

When in English the Indefinite Article follows the Adjective, in such expressions as, *in so short a time*, in Norse the article comes before the adjectival expression, as **i en saa kort Tid**.

en saadan Nar, *such a fool*.
en ganske anden Sag, *quite a different thing*.
han Knut vil endelig ikke samtykke; han er en altfor klog Mand, *he, Knut, will certainly not consent; he is far too wise a man*.

LIST

OF

PHRASES AND IDIOMS.

A.

Able . . . *I have not been able to find an opportunity of telling him*, jeg har ikke kunnet komme til at sige ham.
Absence . . *He was conspicuous by his absence*, han glimrede ved sin Fraværelse.
Accompany *May I accompany you?* maa jeg følge med? *Will you come too?* vil De følge med?
Account for *I cannot account for it*, jeg kan ikke forklare mig det.
Actually . *He is actually going to walk*, han vil absolut gaa tilfods.
Again . . *As big again*, nok saa stor. *Don't mention this to anyone*, ikke mine Ord igjen. *Over and over again*, atter og atter.
Agree . . . *I agree with him in this matter*, jeg er enig med ham om denne Sag.
Ail . . . . *What ails you?* hvad fattes Dem? hvad feiler du?
Alike . . . *All the children are dressed alike*, alle Børnene gaa eensklædte.
All . . . . *When all's said and done*, naar alt kommer til alt. *Nothing at all*, slet intet.
Allow . . . *It is not allowed*, det tillades ikke.
All right . . *It will be all right*, det gaar nok. *Never mind!* aa, bryd Dem ikke!
Ask . . . . *You must ask your way*, du maa spørge dig frem. *May I ask you for the salt*, maa jeg bede Dem om Saltet?
Associate . *To associate with bad company*, at give sig i Fjærd med slette Folk.

Assured . . *You may rest assured that it is true,* De kan være forvist om at det er sandt.

Attempt . . *It is worth while making the attempt,* det er Forsøg værd.

Away . . . *Get away with you!* afsted med dig! *I must away,* jeg maa afsted. *To get away,* at slippe bort. *I shall not be long away,* jeg bliver ikke længe borte. *Money thrown away,* det er bortkastede Penge. *I could not away with Mathematics,* Mathematiken kunde jeg ikke komme afsted med. *Fire away!* snak væk!

B.

Back . . . *We must not speak ill of one behind his back,* vi maa ikke tale ilde om En paa hans Bag. *Backwards and forwards,* frem og tilbage. *He fell on his back,* han faldt om paa Ryggen.

Bad . . . . *That's a bad job,* det er slemt. *He is a bad man,* det er et slet Menneske. *A bad business,* en slem Historie. *A sad dog,* en slem Fyr. *The evil one,* den Slemme. *Bad weather,* daarligt Veir. *Not so bad,* ikke saa Feil. *This is too bad,* det er alt for galt. *Things are going badly with him,* det er galt fat med ham. *Things look bad,* det seer galt ud.

Bargain . . *To strike a bargain,* at afslutte en Handel. *Make a good bargain,* at gjøre en god Handel. At faae for meget godt Kjøb.

Bark . . . *Barking dogs seldom bite,* den Hund som gjør bider ikke.

Be . . . . *I shall be twenty-one to-morrow,* jeg bliver een og tyve Aar imorgen. *Don't be angry,* bliv ikke vred. *It will be difficult,* det bliver vanskeligt. *When will it be?* Naar bliver det? *If it had not been for him,* dersom han ikke var. *That is a different affair,* det var en anden Tale. *He was frightened, and no mistake,* det kan nok være at han blev forskrækket. *According as the weather is,* efter som Veiret er til.

Become . . *What is become of him?* hvor er han bleven af?

Beg . . . . *I beg pardon,* jeg beder om Forladelse. *May I beg you*

LIST OF PHRASES AND IDIOMS. 149

won't do that another time? maa jeg frabede mig det en anden Gang?

Best.... *It will be the best plan*, det bliver det Bedste. *I will use my best endeavours*, jeg skal gjøre min bedst mulige Flid. *He made the best of his way home*, han skyndte sig hjem det Bedste han havde lært. *We must make the best of it*, vi maa benytte det paa det Bedste.

Bet.... *I'll bet you what you like*, jeg vil vædde hvadsomhelst. *Ten to one*, ti mod een. *What will you bet he comes to-day?* hvad gjælder det han kommer idag?

Better... *You had better*, De gjøre bedre i at. *She is no better than she should be*, hun er ikke af Vorherres bedste Børn.

Bit.... *A little bit*, en lille bitte Smule. Et lille Gran. *Not a bit of it*, ikke det bitterste. Skudt forbi!

Bite... *I got a bite*, jeg fik Bid. *I gave him a bone to bite*, jeg gav ham noget at bide paa.

Blow... *The wind blows from that quarter, does it?* blæser Vinden fra den Kant? *Blow upon blow*, Slag i Slag.

Boil... *Will you have the chicken boiled or roasted?* Vil De have Kyllingerne kogt eller stegt? *You must not boil them too much*, De maa ikke forkoge dem. *This is not quite boiled enough*, dette er lidt ikke meget kogt. *They are boiled to shreds*, de ere kogt i Laser.

Book... *The Book of books*, Bøgernes Bog. *Do you book through to Trondhjem?* sælger De gjennemgaaende Billeter til Trondhjem?

Boots... *Puss in boots*, den bestøvlede Kat. *Brush my boots, please*, behag at børste mine Støvler.

Borrow.. *He that goes a borrowing goes a sorrowing*, Borg gjør Sorg.

Breakfast.. *Let us get some breakfast*, lad os faae lidt Frokost.

Breeze... *When there is a light breeze on the water*, naar der lufter lidt paa Vandet.

Brook... *Many small brooks make a large river*, mange Bække smaa gjør en stor Aa.

Business.. *It's no business of mine*, det kommer mig ikke ved. *Mind your own business*, pass Dem selv.

C.

Call . . . . *What is that called in Norwegian?* hvad heder det paa Norsk? *That's what I call singing,* det kalder jeg at synge. *Call off your dog,* kald Hunden til Dem.

Card . . . *To leave a card on one,* at aflægge et Kort hos En.

Care . . . *Take care!* pass paa! Tag dig i Agt! *He does not care a straw for it,* han agter det ikke en Døit værd. *I don't care a jig for him,* jeg blæser ad ham.

Chance . . *By chance,* af en Hændelse. *We must take our chance,* vi maa lade det komme an derpaa.

Change . . *I have not any change,* jeg kan ikke give (Penge) igjen. *Where do we change horses?* hvor skifter man Hestene?

Charge. . *He charged me two crowns for it,* han forlangte to Kroner af mig for det.

Chickens . . *Don't count your chickens before they are hatched,* sælg ikke Bjørnens Hud før du har fanget den.

Child . . . *Children and fools speak the truth,* af Børn og Narre skal man høre Sandheden.

Close . . . *The close season,* den forbudne Tid.

Coals . . . *To carry coals to Newcastle,* at give Bagerbørn Hvedebrød.

Cock . . . *Cock of the walk,* første Hane i Kurven. *The gun is at half cock,* Hanen staar paa Ro, eller, paa halv. *To cock a gun,* at spænde Hanen paa et Gevær.

Comfortable *I am very comfortable here,* jeg har det ganske behageligt her. *Make yourself comfortable,* gjør dig det bekvemt.

Common . . *The common good,* det almindelige Bedste. *The charges are borne in common,* det gaar paa fælles Bekostning.

Concern . . *As far as concerns me,* hvad mig angaar. *It is no concern of yours,* det angaar ikke Dem.

Continue . . *He continued (kept on) walking,* han blev stadig ved at gaae.

Convenient . *Whenever it is convenient to you,* naar det er dem beleiligt.

Course . . . *That is a matter of course,* det følger af sig selv. Det forstaar sig selv.

Custom . . *It is the custom here,* det er her Skik og Brug. *It is not the custom,* det bruges ikke her tillands.

D.

Day . . . . *The whole day*, den hele Dag. *All this day*, i hele Dagen. *Any day*, alle Dage. *One of these days*, en af Dagene. *Next day*, Dagen efter. *This day week*, idag om otte Dage. *Till late in the day*, til højt op paa Dagen.

Death . . . *To be worked to death*, at arbeide sig fordærvet. *To beat to death*, at slaae En ihjel. *It was the death of him*, han tog sin Død derover.

Delve . . . *When Adam delved and Eve span, who was then the gentleman?* da Adam grov og Eva spand, hvor fandtes da en Edelmand?

Depend . . *That depends*, det kommer an paa. *As if his life depended on it*, som om det gjaldt hans Liv.

Difference . *It makes no difference to me*, det er mig uden Forskjel.

Dinner . . . *You'll stay to dinner*, De bliver til Middags. *To take a lady in to dinner*, at føre en Dame tilbords.

Directly . . Nu strax. Ret nu.

Discharge . *He has got his discharge*, han har faaet sin Afsked paa graat Papir.

Do . . . . *Do as the friar saith, not as he doeth*, gjør som Præsten prædiker, og ikke som han handler. *It can't be done*, det lader sig ikke gjøre. *What have you done with the fishing-rod?* hvor har du gjort af Fiskestangen? *What's done can't be undone*, hvad der er skeet kan ei gjøres om. *That will do*, saa er det godt. *That has nothing to do with it*, det hører ikke til Sagen. *Do shut that door*, luk dog den Dør. *Do look*, see dog. *It won't do*, det duer ikke. Det gaar ikke an.

Door . . . *The door flew open*, Døren fløi op. *To knock at a door*, at banke paa Døren. *To shut the door in one's face*, lukke Døren for Næsen af En. *With open doors*, for aabne Døre.

Doubt . . . *I don't doubt you are right*, jeg tvivler ikke paa at De har Ret.

Down . . . *To light one down stairs*, at lyse En ned ad Trapperne.

Drown . . . *He who is born to be hanged will never be drowned*, den drukner ei som hænges skal.

E.

Ear . . . . To set people by the ears, at sætte Folk i Haarene paa hverandre (*the hairs*). *Little pitchers have large ears*, smaa Gryder have ogsaa Øren.

Earnest . . . *You are surely not in earnest*, det er dog ikke Deres Alvor.

Either . . . *I don't care a pin for either of you*, jeg bryder mig ikke en Døit om nogen af Eder.

End . . . . . *All's well that ends well*, naar Enden er god er alting godt.

Energy . . . *There is no energy in him*, der er ingen Drift i ham.

Engage . . . *Well then, I engage him as servant*, saa antager jeg ham i Tjeneste.

Escape . . . *He had a narrow escape*, med Nød og næppe slap han derfra.

Extract . . . *I extracted, fished out of him, where he was going*, jeg fik lokket ud af ham hvor han vilde hen.

F.

Face . . . . *To make faces at one*, at skjære Ansigter ad En. *To say a thing to one's face*, at sige noget i Ens aabne Øine.

Fair . . . . *A fair wind*, føielig Vind. *That is only fair*, det er ikke mere end billigt.

Fare . . . Betaling, eller Kjøreløn. *Bill of fare*, Spiseseddel. *How fares it with him?* hvorledes er det fat med ham?

Fatigue . . *Half dead with fatigue*, halv død af Træthed.

Fault . . . *That's not my fault*, det er ikke min Skyld. *If my memory is not at fault*, hvis ikke min Hukommelse slaar mig Feil.

Fence . . . *Where the fence is lowest all will try to get over*, hvor Gjærdet er lavest ville alle over.

Finger . . *His fingers are itching to begin*, hans Fingre klør efter at begynde. *She can wind him round her finger*, hun snør ham om sin lille Finger.

Fire . . . . *To light the fire*, at tænde Ilden. *The curtain caught fire*, der gik Ild i Gardinet. *To put out a fire*, at slukke Ilden. *There's a fire burning in the store*, det brænder i Ovnen. *Out of the frying-pan into the fire*, at komme

LIST OF PHRASES AND IDIOMS. 153

Fish	af Asken og i Ilden, eller, At komme fra Dynen (*the feather-bed*) i Halmen (*straw*). *Neither fish nor flesh*, hverken Fugl eller Fisk. *To fish in troubled waters*, at fiske i rørt Vande. *Tackle*, Fiskeredskab. *To stock a fish-pond*, at besætte en Fiskedam.
Fool	*A fool and his money are soon parted*, naar Narren kommer tiltorvs faar Kræmmeren Penge. *Not such a fool as he looks*, ikke saa dum som han seer ud. *The foolish Virgins*, de daarlige Jomfruer.
Forget	*I have clean forgotten his name*, jeg har rent glemt hans Navn. *Put by is not forgotten*, gjemt er ikke glemt. *I have forgotten what I was going to say*, jeg er kommen fra det jeg vilde sige.
Freeze	*I sat freezing on the Carriol*, jeg sad og frøs paa Karjolen. *His hands were very cold*, han frøs om Hænderne.
Fresh	*Fresh butter*, friskt Smør. *A fresh-water lake*, en fersk Sø.

G.

Gall	*The saddle galls the horse*, Sadelen bryder Hesten.
Gentleman	*What is he like? he looks like a gentleman*, hvordan seer han ud? han seer ud som en dannet Mand.
Get	*He got his deserts*, han fik sin fortjente Løn. *Where did you get that?* hvor har du faaet fat paa det? *He got a good thrashing*, han fik en Dragt Prygl.
Gift	*One must not look a gift horse in the mouth*, given Hest skal man ikke se i Munden, eller, Man skal ei laste given Gave. *I wouldn't have them at a gift*, jeg vilde ikke have dem til givende. *It was a gift*, jeg har faaet det til Foræring.
Go	*Here goes!* lad gaa! *He's gone*, han er væk. *The gun went off*, Bøssen gik.
Good	*It did him good*, det bekom ham vel. Han fandt sig vel derved. *It does me neither good nor harm*, det gjør mig hverken Gavn eller Skade. *Too much of a good thing*, for meget af det Gode. *It will do you no good*, det vil De ikke have godt af. *Good for the head-ache*,

	det hjælper imod Hovedpine. *Good gracious!* Naa du Alstyrende!
Grass . . .	*While the grass is growing the steed is starving,* Koen dør mens Græsset gror.

H.

Half. . . .	*Half an hour,* en halv Time. *An hour and a half,* halv anden Time. *Two hours and a half,* halvtredie Time.
Hands off! .	Væk med Fingrene! Fingrene af Fadet!
Hard . . .	*That's hard lines,* dette er haardt at gaa paa.
Hark! . . .	Lyt!
Head . . .	*Your head won't save your heels,* hvad man ikke har i Hovedet faar man have i Benene. *I can make neither head nor tail of it,* jeg kan hverken finde ud eller ind. *He took it into his head to use yellow flies,* han fandt paa at bruge gule Fluer.
Heavy . . .	*Feel how heavy this fish is,* løft paa Fisken hvor tung den er.
Help . . .	*I could not help it,* jeg kunde ikke gjøre for det. *I could not help laughing,* jeg kunde ikke bare mig for at le. *Help yourself,* forsyn Dem.
Hold . . .	*To get hold of,* at tage, eller, faae fat paa. *To hold water,* at holde Vand.
Hope . . .	*I hope not,* det vil jeg da ikke haabe. *You got my letter, I hope,* du har dog faaet mit Brev.
Hurry . . .	*Why are you in such a hurry?* hvorfor har De saadan Hast? *He was in no hurry to pay,* han forhastede sig ikke med at betale. *There is no hurry,* der er ingen Hast.

I.

Idea	*I have no idea,* det hav jeg ikke Begreb om.
Ill.	*To take ill,* at tage noget ilde op. *To be taken ill,* at blive syg, at faae Ondt. *It is an ill wind that blows nobody good,* intet er saa galt at det jo er godt for noget.
Intend . . .	*Where do you intend to go?* hvor agter De Dem hen? *He intends mischief,* han har Ondt i Sinde.

LIST OF PHRASES AND IDIOMS. 155

Intimate . . *They are very intimate*, de ere Dus med hinanden.
Irritate . . *It irritated him beyond endurance*, han ærgrede sig gul og grøn.

J.

Jew . . . . *The wandering Jew*, den evige Jøde.
Journey . . *A pleasant journey to you*, lykkelig reise! *He has undertaken a long journey*, han har foretaget sig en lang Reise.
Jump . . . *To jump over a ditch*, at springe over en Grøft.
Just . . . *To have a just idea*, at dømme rigtigt. *That's just the beauty of it*, det er just Dyden derved. *Just look!* Se dog! *Just as I was going to fire*, ret som jeg vilde til at Skyde.

K.

Kind . . . *Be so kind as to show me the way*, vær saa artig, eller, snild, at vise mig Veien.
Knack . . . *He has the knack of it*, han har det rette Greb paa den Sag.
Know . . . *I don't know him*, jeg kjender ham ikke. *Not that I know of*, ikke mig bevidst. Ikke det jeg veed. *He is a knowing fellow*, han veed hvor David kjøbte Øllet. Han kan mere end sin Fader.

L.

Labourer . *The labourer is worthy of his hire*, en Arbeider er sin Løn værd.
Last . . . *When he locked the door the last thing at night*, da han stængte Døren som var det sidste han gjorde om Aftenen. *Thank you for the last time we were together*, Tak for sidst. *Last month*, forrige Maaned. *Here you are at last*, kommer De endelig engang.
Late . . . *I came ten minutes too late*, jeg kom ti Minuter for sent. *Sooner or later*, før eller sildigere.
Laugh . . . *He laughed in my face*, han lo mig op i Ansigtet. *I could not help laughing*, jeg maatte le.
Lease . . . *To lease a river*, at tage en Elv i Forpagtning. *The fishing*

	is taken on a long lease, Fiskeriet er forpagtet paa langt Aaremaal.
Leave . . .	*Leave me at peace,* lad mig være i Fred. *To leave one alone,* at lade En være ene. *Leave this place,* forlad dette Sted. *To take leave of,* tage Afsked med, eller fra. *By your leave,* med Forlov. *He has leave to fish here,* han har Tilladelse til at fiske her.
Leg	*He made good use of his legs,* han tog Benene med sig.
Liberty . .	*I take the liberty to,* jeg tager mig den Frihed at.
Like . . .	*He likes the place,* han liker sig paa dette Sted. *Would you like some coffee?* behager De Kaffe? *How do you like this?* hvorledes behager dette Dem? *Well, I never heard the like of that,* Nei! nu har jeg aldrig hørt Magen dertil. *Like will to like,* lige søger lige. *They are as like as two peas,* de ligne hinanden som to Draaber Vand.
Limit . . .	*One must draw the limit somewhere,* man maa Etsteds sætte en Grændse.
Long . .	*Don't be away long,* bliv ikke længe. *It can't be long since he went,* det kan ikke være længe siden han gik. *I find the time long,* Tiden falder mig lang. *Six inches long,* sex Tommer lang. *We have a long way before us,* det er langt frem.
Look .	*It looks likely to be a good season,* det seer ud til at blive et godt Aar.
Lose .	*I have lost all desire for it,* jeg har tabt Lysten dertil. *Lost the book,* Bogen er mig frakommen. *It is lost labour,* det er spildt Arbeide. *At a loss what to do with oneself,* være forlegen med sig selv.

M.

Mad . . .	*It is enough to drive one mad,* det er til at blive gal over.
Make . . .	*I made her laugh,* jeg fik hende til at le.
Manage . .	*He managed to escape,* han magde det saa at han slap.
Matter. . .	*It does not matter,* det gjør Ingenting. Det er intet at betyde. *I beg your pardon. It doesn't matter,* om Forladelse. Ingen Aarsag. *What's the matter?* hvad er der paa Færde? *There is something wrong,* der er noget galt paa Færde.

LIST OF PHRASES AND IDIOMS. 157

Mean . . . *What does he mean by that?* hvad vil han sige dermed? *What's the meaning of that?* hvad skal det betyde! *I meant no harm*, jeg mente intet Ondt dermed. *I did not mean that*, det var ikke saaledes ment.

Meddle . . *One must not meddle with other people's business*, man maa ikke blande sig i Andres Sager.

Mend . . . *Can you mend this watch?* kan du gjøre ved dette Uhr? *No, it won't stand any more mending*, nei, det lader sig ikke længer istandsættes.

Mention . . *Pray, don't mention it*, Jeg beder.

Mind . . . *To speak one's mind*, at sige sin Mening reent ud.

Miss . . . *He missed it*, det slog glip for ham. *You need not be afraid of his missing the way*, du behøver ikke at være bange for at han vil tage Feil. *To miss the mark*, at skyde Bom.

Morning . . *At ten o'clock in the morning*, Klokken ti om Formiddagen.

Most . . . *That is the way with most people*, saaledes gaar det med de Fleste.

Murder . . *Murder will out*, Mord kan ei dølges.

Must . . . *I suppose I must*, jeg faar vel at gjøre det. *It must be allowed*, det faar være tilladt. *You must stay at home*, du faar blive hjemme.

N.

Name . . . *He sent in his name*, han lod sig melde.

Nap . . . . *To take a nap*, at faae sig et Blund; at tage sig en Lur.

Native . . . *He is a native of England*, han er en født Englænder.

Need . . . *You need not come*, du behøver ikke at komme. *I have no need for it*, jeg har intet Behøv derfor. *I need (take) two hours to get my lesson by heart*, jeg behøver to Timer at lære min Lektie udenad.

Neither . . *Neither of us two*, ingen af os to.

Never . . . *Never is a long word*, man skal aldrig sige aldrig. *Better late than never*, bedre sent end aldrig.

Newspaper . *I will take that newspaper after you, please*, maa jeg see den Avis efter Dem?

Nice . . . *You are a nice fellow*, du er en fet Karl.

No . . . . *No, you don't say so,* Nei dog! *By no means,* aldeles ikke! *Certainly not,* nei, vidst ikke. *It is no go,* det gaar ikke.
Nonsense . Dum Snak!
Not . . . . *Indeed I have not said any such thing,* det har jeg heller ikke sagt. *It has not been asserted ever,* det har heller aldrig været paastaaet. *Not for the world,* ikke for aldrig.
Not till . . *They are not to be married for six months yet,* de skulle først have Bryllup om et halvt Aar.

O.

Oar . . . . *To unship the oar,* at lægge Aarerne ind. *To keep stroke with the oars,* at holde Aaretag.
Oath . . . *I will take my oath of it,* jeg vil gjøre min Ed derpaa.
Objection . *If you have no objection,* naar De har intet derimod. *I have no objection,* for mig gjærne.
Odds and Ends . . . Dit og Dat. *It makes no odds to me,* det er mig uden Forskjel.
Off . . . . *Hands off!* bort med Fingrene! *Off with you!* afsted med dig! *The letter was sent off,* Brevet afgik. *Off hand,* rask væk.
Old . . . . *As the old cock crows so cackle the young,* som de gamle sjunge, saa kviddre de Unge. *For old times' sake,* for Gammels Skyld.
On . . . . *Drive on!* kjør til! *We must trudge on foot,* vi maa reise med Apostolenes Heste.
Only . . . *He arrived only half an hour ago,* han kom først for en halv Time siden. *Only hear what I have to say,* saa hør dog hvad jeg vil sige.
Open . . . *Leave the door open,* lad Døren staa aaben. *Open air,* den frie Luft.
Opinion . . *In my opinion,* efter min Mening.
Opportunity *I let the opportunity go by,* jeg lod Leiligheden gaae forbi.
Own . . . . *He won't own that he has written,* han vil ikke være bekjendt at han har skrevet. *He has a house of his own,* han har sit eget Hus.

LIST OF PHRASES AND IDIOMS. 159

P.

Pack . . . *Pack one's things up*, at pakke Tøiet ind. *Pack off!* Pak dig! *The grouse had begun to pack*, Ryperne havde begyndt at flokke sig.

Pains . . . *He took great pains*, han gjorde sig megen Flid.

Pardon . . *I beg you a thousand pardons*, jeg beder tusinde Gange om Forladelse.

Part . . . *For the most part*, for den største Del.

Pay . . . . *How much to pay?* hvor meget at betale? *You shall pay for this*, dette skal du komme at betale. *He shall be paid off (atone)*, han skal ikke dø i Synden.

Penny . . . *In for a penny, in for a pound*, har man sagt A, maa man sige B.

Pins . . . *A paper of pins*, et Brev Knappenaal. *One could almost hear a pin fall*, man kunde næsten høre en Knappenaal falde.

Please . . . *Sit down, please*, behag at tage Plads. *As you please*, efter Behag, eller, som De behager.

Poison . . *One man's meat is another man's poison*, Een Mands Brød anden Mands Død.

Positively . *I positively won't wait any longer*, jeg vil tilforladelig ikke vente længer.

Post . . . . *By this day's post*, med Posten idag. *For the next post*, med omgaaende Post. *To deliver a letter at the Post Office*, at aflevere et Brev paa Posthuset, eller, Postaabneri. *Postage stamp*, et Frimærke.

Pretend . . *He pretended that he was an Englishman*, han anstillede sig som om han var Engelskmand.

Promise . . *To keep one's promise*, at holde hvad man har lovet.

Providence . *There is a providence that takes care of fools*, Vorherre er alle Daarers Formynder.

Put by . . . *He had put by something for a rainy day*, han havde lagt sig noget til Bedste.

Q.

Quench . . *Give me a drink of water to quench my thirst*, giv mig et Drik Vand at læske mig paa.

Quits . . . *Double or quits*, kvit eller dobbelt.

R.

Race	Væddeløb. *Boat race,* Kaproning. *Sail race,* Kapseilads.
Reason	*What was the reason of his not coming?* af hvad Aarsag kom han ikke?
Remember	*To the best of my remembrance,* saa vidt jeg kan erindre. *I called to remembrance,* det randt mig ihu. *Remember me to your mother,* hils Moderen fra mig.
Responsibility	*He did it on his own responsibility,* han gjorde det paa sit eget Ansvar og Tilsvar.
Rid of	*He wants to get rid of her,* han vil blive af med hende. *To get rid of,* at blive noget Kvit.
Roads	*It is a two hours' drive when the roads are in good condition,* i godt Føre kjører man Veien paa to Timer.

S.

Salvation	*The Salvation Army,* Frelsens Armee.
Scot-free	*Let him go scot-free,* kald ham graa og lad ham gaa.
Sense	*Common sense,* den sunde Fornuft. *He is not in his right senses,* han er ikke ved sin fulde Fem.
Serve	*That won't serve my turn,* det kan jeg ikke være tjent med. *It serves him right,* det har han godt af.
Settle	*That settled the question,* dermed var Sagen afgjort. *It was a settled plan between them,* det var et aftalt Spil imellem dem.
Share	*To share good luck and bad,* at staa Last og Brast med En.
Sharp	*Look sharp!* skynd dig! *You need not be so sharp upon one,* De tør ikke være saa bidende.
Shift	*One can make shift with it at a pinch,* til Nød kan man vel hjælpe sig dermed.
Shoot	*To shoot dead,* at skyde ihjel. *To be out shooting,* være paa Jagt.
Shut	*Shut the door,* luk Døren. *To shut one out,* at lukke En ude. *To let one out,* at lukke En ud.
Sight	*Out of my sight,* bort fra mit Aasyn! *Sight of a gun,* Sigtekornet.
Signify	*It does not signify,* det er intet at betyde.
Silk-purse	*You can't make a silk-purse out of a sow's ear,* man skal

LIST OF PHRASES AND IDIOMS. 161

	længe hygge paa en Elletrunke inden man faar en Bisværm deraf.
Slippery . .	. *As slippery as an eel*, glat som en Aal. *Slippery walking*, glat at gaae.
Sneeze . . .	. *It is not to be sneezed at*, det er ikke Grød at grine ad.
Song . . .	. *As the old song has it*, som det heder i Visen.
Sorts . . .	. *I am out of sorts to-day*, jeg er ikke rask idag, eller, rigtig i mit Es idag. *She is out of sorts*, hun er ikke i sit Es.
Spare . . .	. *It is too late to spare when the bottom is bare*, det er bedre at spare paa Bredden end paa Bunden.
Stay . . .	. *How long did you stay there?* hvor længe blev du der? *Stay here*, bliv her. *To make a couple of days' stay*, at ligge over et Par Dage.
Stop . . .	. *Stop that!* Aa, lad være! *We stop here five minutes*, fem Minuters Ophold her. *To stop talking*, at holde op med at snakke.
Strange . .	. *Strange to say*, besynderligt nok. *I am a stranger here*, jeg er fremmed her. *They are entire strangers*, de ere vilde Fremmede.
Stream . .	. *To go down stream*, at seile nedad Floden. *A strong stream*, or *current*, en stærk Strøm.
Supper . .	. *What shall we have for supper?* hvad skal vi have til Aftens? *Stay to supper*, bliv og spiis Aftens hos os.
Suspicion .	. *I had no suspicion there was anything amiss*, jeg havde ingen Anelse om at der var noget galt.
Swear . . .	. *He swears like a trooper*, han bander som en Tyrk.
Swell . . .	. *He sets up for a swell*, han paatager sig et fornemt Væsen, eller, han bilder sig ind at være fornem.

T.

Table .	. *To keep a good table*, at føre et godt Bord. *Clear away table*, at tage af Bordet. *Dinner is on the table*, Maden er paa Bordet. *To say grace*, at læse tilbords.
Talk . . .	. *He talks Norwegian*, han snakker, eller, taler Norsk. *That is mere talk*, det er bare Snak. *Too much talk brings regret*, af megen Tale kommer Fortrydelse.
Taste . . .	. *That's quite to his taste*, det falder ganske i hans Smag.
Think . . .	. *I thought as much*, det tænkte jeg nok.

M

Thorough . He got a thorough wetting, han blev dygtig vaad. A thorough good thrashing, han fik dygtig Bank.
Throw . . . The horse threw his rider, Hesten slog Rytteren af.
Time . . . A stitch in time saves nine, Forsorg ere bedre end Eftersorg.
Tongue . . I have it on the tip of my tongue, det ligger mig paa Tungen.
Too bad . . It is really too bad, det er dog for galt.
Trace . . . Not the least trace, ikke mindste Spor.
Trouble . . Oh, don't trouble, aa, bryd Dem ikke. After no end of bother and trouble, efter syv Sorger og otte Bedrøvelser.
Try . . . . To try on a pair of shoes, at passe et Par Sko. Take on trial, tage paa Prøve. I will try, jeg skal probere. To try one's hand at, forsøge sig i.
Try . . . . He will not try that on again, han vil ikke prøve paa det oftere. Try a pair of gloves, at passe, eller, prøve, et Par Handsker.

U.

Undertake . Whatever he undertook failed, alt hvad han foretog sig, slog Feil.
Undress . . At klæde sig af.
United . . The United States, de forenede Stater.

V.

Visit . . . I am only on a visit here, jeg er kun paa Besøg her.

W.

Wait . . . Wait a bit! bi lidt! Everything comes to the man who can wait, biende Mand faar Bør.
Walk . . . To be a good walker, være rask til Fods.
Wall . . . To drive a nail into the wall, at slaa et Søm i Væggen.
Warning . Let this be a warning to you, lad dette tjene dig til Advarsel.
Way . . . That's not the way of it, det er ikke saaledes fat.
Welcome . Take it, you are quite welcome, ja, vær saa god, eller, saa

LIST OF PHRASES AND IDIOMS. 163

	artig. *You are welcome to leave*, det staar dem frit at drage bort.
Well . . .	*That's all very well*, det er brav nok. *Too late to fill up the well after the child is drowned*, det er for seent at kaste Brønden til naar Barnet et druknet.
What . . .	*I'll tell you what*, veed du hvad? *What noise was that!* hvad var det for en Støi.
Wink at . .	*At se igjennem Fingrene med.*
Wonder . .	*I wonder if he is still alive?* mon han lever endnu? *Where does he live I wonder?* hvor mon han boer?
Word . . .	*I sent him word by my servant*, jeg lod ham sige ved min Tjener.
Work . . .	*To keep one hard at work*, at holde En strengt til Arbeide.
Worse . . .	*So much the worse*, desværre.
Worth . . .	*It is not worth your while*, det er ikke Umagen værdt for Dem.
Wrong . .	*He was not far wrong*, han tog ikke meget Feil. *Unless my memory is wrong*, hvis ikke min Hukommelse slaar mig Feil. *The clock is wrong*, Klokken gaar galt. *What is there wrong in it?* hvad galt er det i det?

Y.

Year . . .	*This year*, i Aar. *Last year*, forrige Aar. *Next year*, næste Aar, eller, Aaret efter. *This day twelve months*, idag om et Aar.
Yore . . .	*Of yore*, i Fordums Tid.
You there! .	*You there!* De der! *Who's there?* hvem der?
Young . .	*One cannot expect old heads on young shoulders*, Ungdom og Viisdom følges sjelden ad.

APPENDIX I.

Epistolary Forms.

The following specimens will show the forms commonly used in letter writing.

I. Between relations and friends. The Adjectives may be varied, of course, according to the degrees of intimacy or affection.

Kjære Datter!
  Som jeg nu staar i Begreb at skrive mit Nytaarsbrev til dig . . . o.s.v. . . . Saa være Gud med dig og dine, kjære Barn!
       Din hengivne,
          Moder.

Kjære Søster!
  Med stor Glæde har jeg modtaget Underretningen om din Forlovelse. &c. &c. . . . Hils ham rigtig hjertelig fra mig, og modtag selv de hjerteligste Hilser fra din.
      Oprigtige Broder,
         Erik.

Min kjære Søn!
  Til Festen imorgen af din Fødselsdag maa vel ogsaa din Fader indfinde sig med sin Lykønskning . . . &c. Og nu lev vel, min Gut, til Glæde,
     for din trofaste Fader,
      Lars Nielsen Birkeland.

Kjæreste Fader!
  Efterretningen om din Sygdom voldte mig stor Bekymring, &c. &c. . . . Altsaa fremdeles god Bedring, kjære Fader!
       din hengivne Søn,
         Anders.

Kjære Ven!
  Med stor Glæde har jeg erfaret at De netop er bleven befordret, og det paa en meget fordelagtig maade, &c. &c. &c.
                    Deres hengivne Ven,
                              PEDER ØLSEN.

Kjære Veninde!
  Jeg kan ikke lade den Høitidsdag gaa forbi uden at have ønsket dig alt det gode et Menneske kan nyde her i Livet, &c. &c. . . . Saa lev vel til vi sees, og tænk undertiden paa,
                    din hengivne Veninde,
                              RAGNHILD SØVIG.

Other forms of address and subscription in familiar letters are—
  Dyrbare Ven!
        .   .   .   .
                    din trofaste Ven,
                              KRISTEN LARSSEN.

Kjæreste Katrina!
        .   .   .   .   .
                              din,
                                    SIGRID.

Kjære Ven!
        .   .   .   .   .   .
                    Deres oprigtige Ven,
                              SØREN PEDERSEN.

Min kjære Hans!
        .   .   .   .
                              din,
                                    ANDERS.

Kjære Ven!
        .   .   .   .
                    Jeg er som altid,
                    Deres oprigtige Ven,
                              DANIEL AASE.

II. Where less familiarity is intended the following expressions are used.

Kjære Fru Nærland!
Tusen Tak for Udførelsen af Kommissionerne, &c. &c. Med mango Hilsener til Dem og Deres, er jeg,
>> Deres hengivne,
>> INGEBORG KALLEM.

Kjære Frøken Mellø!
. . . .
Med den mest spændte Forventning imødeser jeg Deres Svar.
>> Deres hengivne,
>> ELIAS HAMMAR.

Frøken Marit Andersen!
. . . .
>> med Agtelse,
>> Deres trofast hengivne,
>> N. BLIKSTAD.

Kjære Hr. Kjeldsberg!
. . . . . .
>> Deres,
>> KARL AUNE.

Herr Lundgrin!
. . . . .
>> med Agtelse,
>> MARIUS ABREBO.

Kjære Fru Holberg!
Til min store Glæde fandt jeg idag da jeg kom hjem, en Billet, hvori De indbyder mig til at deltage i den Familiefest som snart skal finde Sted i Deres Hjem, &c. &c. Jeg vil derfor ganske sikkert indfinde mig paa den af Dem fastsatte Dag.
>> med Agtelse,
>> Deres hengivne,
>> LEONORA ULFELDT.

III. The following forms are usual where more ceremony or respect is to be observed.

Min Herre!
   De kan ikke blive forundret over at jeg ikke længer kalder Dem Ven, &c. &c. &c.

Ærbødigst,
JOHANN NORDAL BRUN.

Ærede Hr. Grundtvig.
   Jeg maa meget beklage at uforudseede Omstændigheder gjør at jeg ikke ser mig istand at afgjøre, &c. &c.

Ærbødigst,
ENOK MUNCH.

Ærede Hr. Doktor!
   Deres omhyggelige Tilsyn har bevirket at jeg nu føøler mig saa vel at, &c. &c. &c.

Deres taknemmelige Skyldner,
JØRGEN MOE.

Høistærede!
   Af min Ven Henrik Anker's Skrivelse ser jeg at, &c. &c.
med Agtelse forbliver jeg,
Deres Arbødige,
MAURITS HANSEN.

Ærede Hr. Bjerregaard!
   . . . .

Deres Ærbødige Tjener,
JONAS LIE.

IV. Letters to officials.

Til M. N.
   . . . Magistrat eller Foged ell. Lendsmand ell. Konsul.
   Herved tillader jeg mig at anmelde, &c. &c.

Ærbødigst,
PETER ASBJØRNSEN.

den 2ode Juni, 1892.

APPENDIX I.

V. Letters on business.

Hr. N. P.
    Herved tillader jeg mig at meddele, &c. &c.
                                        Ærbødigst,
                                                        P. P.
den 18de November, 1891.

Til Hr. Baggesen,
    .   .   .   .
                    Œrbødigst (eller) med Agtelse,
                                            NILS RENAA.

APPENDIX II.

Norwegian and Danish.

The following passage taken from Bjørnson's 'På Guds Veje,' will illustrate certain points of spelling and pronunciation in which Norwegian differs from Danish.

Edvard gik foran og i dype tanker; den andre efter med løpen.
Her, hvor **bærget tok** av, hørtes havduren, som kom den fra luften; som susen **av** et henover dragende følge, men **svært** høit oppe. Nu blev det koldt; **månen sås**, men **ænnu** ikke **stjærnene**; jo, en enkelt. 'Hvorledes kom du **på** det der?' **spurte** Edvard, han vendte sig; Ole stanset også. Han sendte løpen fra den ene **hånd** over i den **andre** og **tilbake igen**; skulde han kaste sig **ut** i det og sige alt? Edvard forstod straks, at her stak mere under, og at dette var det vigtigste. 'Kan du ikke si det?' **spurte** han, som var det ham **likegyldigt**.—'Jo, jeg kan nok;' men han blev ved at flytte løpen fra **hånd** til **hånd uten** at sige mere. Så kunde Edvard ikke længre dy sig, men gav sig rigtig til at nøde Ole, og det **likte** denne nokså godt; men betænkte sig **ænda**. 'Ja, det er da vel ikke noget **lejt**?'—'Nei, **lejt** er det ikke.' Han la til om en stund; 'Så er det heller noget stort, da,—ja, rigtig noget stort også.'— 'Noget rigtig stort?'—'**Egenlig** er det det største i **værden**.'—'Men **kære dig da**?'—'Ja, når du bare ikke vil fortælle det? Ikke til et liv, **skønner** du? Så kan jeg nok **si** det.'—'Hvad er det, Ole?'—'Jeg vil være missjonær.'—'Missjonær—?!'—'Ja, hedninge-missjonær, rent **ut** for de **ville**, skønner du; **slike**, som spiser folk.' Han så, at Edvard **næppe** kunde **tale** mere; derfor skyndte han sig at lægge til noget om cykloner, rasende rovdyr og giftige slanger. '**Mot slikt må** en øve sig op, ser du.'—'Øve sig op—? **Mot** rasende rovdyr og giftige slanger—?' Edvard **begynte** at tro alting muligt.—'Mænneskene er de værste,' sa Øle, han bøjde **unna** for dyrene;—'de er forfærdelige hedninger, **de folka**, og **sinte** og grumme og **leje** er de også, så de er nok ikke å løpe til. En må nok ha øvelse.'—'Men hvorledes kan du **få** den der **nere**?

De er da ikke hedninger, de der nere i fiskerbyen?'—'Nej, men de kan nok lære **en å tåle lit af hvært**, de; **en** får ikke **gi** sig over der nere; men ta på sig det mest **svinske**. Når de er **syke** og vrange, så er de også så mistænksomme; ja, somme er rigtig **nogen lejels**. Tænk, her en **kvællen** vilde en slå til mig!—**Sla** til d:g!'—'Jeg bad så gud, at hun måtte; men hun **bante** bare.' Øles øjne **tindret**, hans ansigt var i henrykkelse. 'Det **står** i en traktat, jeg har her i løpen, at det er fejlen med vore missjonærer, at de **går** til det **uten å ha** øvet sig op. For det er en **svær** kunst å **vinne** folk, står der; å **vinne** dem for guds **rike** er den **sværeste** af alle kunster; **egenlig** burde vi øve os **pa** det fra unge, ja fra barn **av**; således står der, og det vil jeg **gøre**. For det å være missjonær, ser du, er nu det højeste på jorden **likevel**. Større **æn å være** konge, større **æn å** være kejser og pave; det står her i traktaten. Det står, at en missjonær **sa**: om jeg **hadde** ti liv, jeg gav dem alle ti til missjonen. Det vil jeg **gøre**, jeg også.'

For dybe, *deep.*
„ den anden, *the other.*
„ Bjerget, *the mountain.*
„ tog af, *ended.*
„ Bulder, *roar,* also *written* Tur, Duur.
„ meget, *very.*
„ Maanen, *the moon.*
„ sanes, *was seen.*
„ endnu, *yet.*
„ Stjernerne, *the stars.*
„ paa, *upon.*
„ spurgte, *asked.*
„ idet han vendte sig, *as he turned.*
„ standsede, *stopped.*
„ tilbage igjen, *back again.*
„ ud, *out with it.*
„ sige (infinit), *tell.*
„ ligegyldigt, *a matter of indifference.*
„ nden, *without.*
„ længer, længere, *longer.*

For syntes nok saa godt om, *liked just as well.*
„ endda, *yet further.*
„ let, *light, not heavy.*
„ lagde til, *added.*
„ egentlig, *precisely.*
„ Verden, *world.*
„ bryder du dig derom? *but do you care about it?*
„ skjønner, *do you understand.*
„ Vilde, *wild men, savages.*
„ slige, *such.*
„ neppe, *hardly.*
„ taale, *bear.*
„ mod sligt maa man, *against such one must.*
„ begyndte, *began.*
„ sagde, *said.*
„ bøiede undaf, *bent aside from.*
„ Folk, *those people.*
„ vrede, *angry, ill-tempered.*
„ lede, *nasty, loathsome.*
„ at løbe til, *to come near.*

For dernede, *down there.*
,, man at taale lidt af hvert, *teach one to endure a little of everything.*
,, give, *give.*
,, tage, *take.*
,, svinagtige, *swinish.*
,, syge, *sick and cross.*
,, lejels, *nuisance.*
,, en Kveld, *one evening.*
,, slaae, *strike.*
,, bandte, *only swore.*

For tindrede, *glittered.*
,, uden at have, *without having trained.*
,, vanskelig, *difficult.*
,, at vinde, *to win over.*
,, Rige, *kingdom*
,, gjøre, *do.*
,, sagde, *said.*
,, havde ti Liv vilde jeg give dem *if I had ten lives I would give them all.*

www.ingramcontent.com/pod-product-compliance
Lightning Source LLC
Chambersburg PA
CBHW020846160426
43192CB00007B/805